Listen! God Is Calling!
Luther Speaks of Vocation, Faith, and Work

LUTHERAN
VOICES

Listen! God Is Calling!
Luther Speaks of Vocation, Faith, and Work

D. Michael Bennethum

Augsburg Fortress
Minneapolis

OTHER LUTHERAN VOICES TITLES

Large-quantity purchases or custom editions of these books are available at a discount from the publisher. For more information, contact the sales department at Augsburg Fortress, Publishers, 1-800-328-4648, or write to: Sales Director, Augsburg Fortress, Publishers, P.O. Box 1209, Minneapolis, MN 55440-1209.

See www.lutheranvoices.com

Dedicated to all the committed Christians through the years who have taught me what it means to treat daily work as a holy calling.

LISTEN! GOD IS CALLING!
Luther Speaks of Vocation, Faith, and Work

Editor: Mark Hinton

Cover Design: Koechel Peterson and Associates, Inc., Minneapolis, MN
                www.koechelpeterson.com

Cover photo: Koechel Peterson and Associates, Inc., Minneapolis, MN

ISBN 0-8066-4991-7

Manufactured in the U.S.A.

07   06   05   3   4   5   6   7   8   9   10

Contents

Preface

And whatever you do, in word or deed, do everything in the name of the Lord Jesus, giving thanks to God the Father through him.

(Colossians 3:17 NRSV)

The following true story, by David Dycus, is told in the "All in a Day's Work" column of the *Reader's Digest*:

> I was once a messenger at the photo lab where I work. As I was leaving the building one day, I was paged on my beeper. Instructed to pick up a package at an unfamiliar company with a 12 syllable, tongue twisting name, I looked skyward and said, "God, where am I supposed to go?" Just then my pager came on again, this time with the client's address. A man nearby witnessed this scene. Raising his arms to heaven, he cried, "Why don't you ever answer me?"[1]

The truth is that God does have a word for people that can guide and bring meaning to their daily routines. The trick is knowing how to listen for that word.

In each of the congregations I have served as pastor, it has been my experience that many members have little practical sense of how to connect the faith they profess with the lives they lead. Typically, they have a vague sense that God wants them to live morally upright lives. They hope, of course, that nonbelievers will do the same. They appreciate God's promise of forgiveness, particularly when they have a sense that they have failed. Trying times drive them to prayer. Otherwise, they find comfort in the knowledge that they are "as good as most and better than some." When it comes to the routines of daily life and work, however, their faith as Christians, expressed eagerly in worship and church-related activities, just doesn't seem to play much of a conscious role. *Listen! God Is Calling!* is an attempt to understand why this is so and to propose a resource from the church's heritage that I have found helpful for bridging the gap that exists between Sunday worship and weekday living among so many of today's church members.

In the first two chapters, I make comments and draw conclusions regarding the tendency to separate faith and daily work, noting how this tendency hinders the church's mission to be a transforming presence in the world. In doing so, I draw on my own observations from almost twenty-five years as a parish pastor and on my reading of sociologists of religion, theologians, and other concerned observers of the church.

Some of these observers have suggested that a renewed emphasis on the traditional Lutheran teaching regarding the vocation of all the baptized can again be a useful tool for helping Christians bridge the gap. Building on this suggestion, Chapters 3 and 4 offer an overview of the church's understanding of vocation, focusing particularly on Martin Luther's redefinition of the term.

It is important for the reader to recognize that Luther's teaching, while truly revolutionary in his day, was conditioned by the culture in which he lived. Luther, with his down-to-earth style of writing, used concrete (and, from the point of view of the twenty-first century, stereotypical) examples of what it means for a husband or wife or servant or noble or commoner to express his or her call from God in daily life and work. Readers must be able to look beyond certain time-bound assumptions to appreciate what Luther is affirming regarding the dignity of the honorable work of all God's people.

I have taken care to select direct quotations that will pose a minimum of stumbling blocks for the reader. When this is not possible, I have left the quotations as they were written, rather than edit out descriptions that may offend. Nor do I make corrections for gender specific language pertaining to people and to God.

Language, of course, is important in shaping thought. One area in which I struggle with language regards references to the vast majority of church members whose primary arena for work is away from the church building. Traditionally, these members have been called lay people or the laity. From the Greek *laos* (people), these terms originally referred to the whole people of God. Today, they have a more negative connotation, denoting those who are presumed to be untrained or unskilled in a particular field of endeavor. Such a meaning runs counter to the sense of value that the teaching on vocation ascribes to all productive endeavor. For that reason, I avoid the term lay person wherever possible, writing instead about the baptized or believers or, simply, Christians.

One of my presuppositions is that meaningful change—whether individual or institutional—occurs in small, manageable steps that are reinforced through a variety of strategies. Chapter 5 presents suggestions for reorienting practices in several areas of congregational life as a way of reclaiming the power of Luther's teaching on vocation as an inspirational tool for integrating faith and work.

I am convinced that as Western society continues on its path of ever greater secularism and ever broader pluralism, the task of encouraging believers to be more intentional about relating Sunday to Monday will be an essential component in maintaining the vitality of the church. The final chapter restates the urgency and the difficulty of this task. It also celebrates the positive impact that the teaching on vocation has had for those church members who have learned to apply it to the particular contexts of their lives, viewing their daily activities from the perspective of their faith in God's active presence in the world.

This book would not have been possible without the encouragement and critical feedback I received from Eric Heen,

Timothy Wengert, and Paul Spohn—the readers of my doctor of ministry project on which this book is based. I also thank Carol Weiser, William Diehl, Sally Simmel, and Bob Sitze—for awakening in me a deeper understanding of the power of the Christian faith for everyday life and work.

1

The Sunday–Monday Split

To maintain spiritual integrity, we need a spirituality that integrates,
not separates, our faith and work.

   <✍> *Gordon Preece[1]*

Recently, I asked participants in an adult study session to work
in small groups to create two collages. The first was to represent
how they are involved in the life and ministry of our congregation.
The second was to depict ways in which they serve God away
from the church building. I was not surprised when I looked over
the first set of collages. The pieces of poster board overflowed with
pictures, symbols, phrases, and drawings of singing choirs, folks
kneeling in prayer, busy committees, people pruning hedges, and
adults teaching children. I was disappointed to discover that the
second set of collages was little different from the first, except in
one way—the location of the actions being depicted. Every word
and picture on those second sheets of poster board referred to
church-sponsored activities that took place away from our building and campus—people serving a meal at a homeless shelter or
hammering in nails at a Habitat for Humanity project. The members of the study group could not, it seemed, think of service to
God apart from their involvement in the ministries of the church.

Since that time, I have encountered similar thinking again and
again as I have spoken to congregational teams from around the
country at SPLASH! events. *SPLASH! Ripples of the Baptized* is
an emphasis of the Evangelical Lutheran Church in America
(ELCA) designed to assist congregations in encouraging their
members to relate the faith they profess on a Sunday morning to
all of their Monday through Saturday activities and relationships.

Even the pastors and congregation members motivated enough to participate in the SPLASH! training program struggle to envision ways in which service to God can happen beyond the context of church-sponsored programs.

In 1972, Richard Avery and Donald Marsh wrote a folk song that was to become a favorite among members of my college Christian fellowship group: "We Are the Church." The lyrics to the refrain read:

"I am the church! You are the church!

We are the church together!

All who follow Jesus, all around the world!

Yes, we're the church together."

The first verse of the song states a well-known Christian principle:

"The church is not a building, the church is not a steeple,

The church is not a resting place, the church is a people!"[2]

Words: Richard Avery & Donald Marsh
© 1972 Hope Publishing Co, Carol Stream, IL 60188.
All right reserved. Used by permission.

Indeed, the church is not a building. It is a people. That insight has been quoted so often as to qualify it as a truism. However, it has been my experience that all too many Christians think of the church as the people *in* the building or at least as people who are doing church-related things. They appreciate quality worship, inspiring music, and effective preaching. They are convinced of the value of the various educational and social ministry projects that their congregations undertake. There is no doubt in their minds that these activities are the work of the church, the community of God's people.

They are, of course, "the church together." But these same believers need to be reminded that they are also the church when they are not together. They are the baptized people of God, bearers of the good news of Jesus, even when they are far from one another—scattered in their daily places, doing their mundane, everyday activities. Most Christians, even the most eager volunteers, spend far more time engaging in their chores and relationships at home, in their daily work, and even in their favorite recreational pursuits than they do participating in the activities of their congregations. Many of them, however, have little conscious sense that the things they are doing far away from the church building, far away from the church's rituals and programs, far away from other congregational members are also the work of the church. They are surprised when they are told that there is a connection between what they sing and say and do with their fellow believers on Sunday and what they do during the rest of their week.

There are many reasons why this insight is not self-evident to more Christians. These will be explored in greater depth in the next chapter. One of the most obvious reasons for the Sunday–Monday split is vocabulary. The institutional church speaks a different language than that which most people speak in the course of their daily lives. "Churchy" words—such as pew, narthex, kingdom, kyrie—suggest that the church deals with a reality all its own.

Another issue lies in the allocation of resources. Congregations can be very busy places. Amid the never-ending task of recruiting willing volunteers to attend to the in-house needs of the church as institution and to staff the myriad projects and activities sponsored by most congregations, there is little energy or motivation to affirm the importance of faithful Christian living in other arenas, except in the most general of terms. Pastors and associates in ministry can become so focused on the ministries of the gathered church that they have scant understanding of the issues and concerns, the priorities and challenges that the average weekday poses for the Christian. It is not surprising, then, that many believers assume that the church has no interest in and their faith has no role to play in dealing with those issues and concerns, priorities and challenges.

Nelvin Vos, in his article, "The Vocation of the Laity," speaks about Christians who celebrate the real presence of Christ at the altar, but who have come to assume "the doctrine of the real absence at the desk and assembly line and the kitchen sink."[3] In her book, *All God's People Are Ministers*, Patricia Page quotes the reflections of a lay church member:

> "So far I have worked out my Christianity at work unaided. There are no obvious forums for discussion, or at least when they exist they rarely touch the workplace."[4]

The faith of the church has something to say to folks in the ordinary, mundane, secular world in which they live. Christian living is meant to embrace a rhythm between gathering and scattering, between life together in a congregation and life apart engaged in the hodgepodge of activities that make up a person's daily routine. In both locations, baptized believers are the church and the things they do are expressions of what they believe.

Corporate worship, word and sacrament ministry, on-going Christian education, and the service ministries of the church are not intended to be elements of an isolated spiritual sphere, neatly compartmentalized away from the secular life of the Christian. They do not constitute merely the offer of a respite or an escape from the stresses of everyday living. Yet, that is the limit of what many church members look for in their gathering times. A central goal of the gathered community of faith—whether it has come together for worship, for education, or for fellowship—ought to be to prepare the baptized to return to their weekday activities with renewed energy and clearer perspective, even as the incongruities and frustrations of those weekday activities drive the baptized back to the sustenance offered in the gathered Christian community.

It is important for pastors and other congregational leaders to be as effective as they possibly can be in assisting members to appreciate this rhythm, this connection between life among fellow believers in the community of faith and life apart from them the rest of the week—for it is not self-evident to most of the baptized that they are the church in both of these locations. Equipping members to listen for God's call as it applies to the large portion of their lives spent away from the church's building and programs should be a priority for ministry.

When this happens, it leads to two important benefits. First, individual Christians appreciate and make greater use of the resources of their faith (that is, their personal piety) and their church membership (that is, their participation in the life of the gathered community) as avenues through which they can both celebrate the satisfactions of daily living and receive support for dealing with its stresses. They feel less alone as they cope with the challenges of their weekday lives, knowing that there, too, God is present with them and that there is a body of fellow believers who care about them and the things with which they must occupy themselves in the course of a busy day.

Second, there is a benefit for the mission of the church. Congregations are able to multiply their potential for making an impact on the larger community, since this impact no longer depends solely on their officially sponsored ministries. The church's call to repentance, offer of forgiveness and new beginnings, and promise of God's love and acceptance find tangible expression in the lives and attitudes and witness of all of its members as they go about their routine activities in the various places in which they spend their time in the course of a week.

There is nothing novel in this insight. The following statement was made at the Evanston Assembly of the World Council of Churches in 1954:

> The time has come to make the ministry of the laity explicit, visible and active in the world. The real battles of the faith today are being fought in factories, shops, offices and farms, in political parties and government agencies, in countless homes, in the press, radio and television, in the relationship of nations. Very often it is said that the church should "go into these spheres"; but the fact is, that the church is already in these spheres in the persons of its laity.[5]

Over the past half century since this statement was made, dozens of books, articles, and courses of study have been written for the purpose of bridging the gap that exists in the minds of many church members between faith and ordinary life. These writings endeavor to address the perceived lack of connection between institutional church activity and the activities of daily living. In spite of these many and often passionate works, the gap remains—such are the inertial forces that foster it.

One of the ongoing struggles of those at the forefront of a "faith and daily life" movement has been to identify a vocabulary that will encourage Christian individuals and congregations to explore more intentionally the relationship between what they profess in worship and what they do the rest of the week. Words have a great deal of power. How we understand certain terms can affect our attitudes.

Many authors write about believers having a "ministry" in daily life. Their hope is to hold up this English translation of the Greek term *diakonia* (service) as a reminder that all the baptized can render service to God through the whole of their lives. The difficulty with using this term lies in the fact that most American Christians associate it with people employed in paid church positions (pastors who, in many denominations, are called ministers, associates in ministry, ministers of music, etc.) While *minister* has religious connotations in North America, in many countries the term conjures up the image of a person who holds a governmental office.

Other writers promote Martin Luther's assertion that all Christians are members of a "universal priesthood of believers" as a way of encouraging the baptized to consider the role their faith can play in the conduct of daily living. Priest, however, is a word with such a long history of cultic usage that it is difficult to disassociate it from its liturgical connotations. Also, Luther's original assertion that every Christian can function as a priest toward his or her neighbors; that is, as an intermediary between those neighbors and God, has often been perverted in our individualistic culture to mean that every Christian, as a priest, has immediate access to God and, therefore, needs no intermediary. This obscures the community-enhancing function of Luther's original declaration.

In my pastoral and educational ministry, I have experimented with another term—*vocation*. This, too, has a significant history of usage in the church, and its meaning has changed through the centuries. In the Reformation of the sixteenth century, Martin Luther's radical redefinition of this term became a source of inspiration for many Christians. Today, however, it is seldom used among protestant Christians, except in the general, societal sense of a synonym for occupation.

It has been my experience that it is possible to reclaim the richness of this word—the Latinized translation of the New Testament term for "calling." Time and again I have observed that when adults in the church discover that God has *called them* to let their faith as Christians permeate every aspect of their lives, they internalize this insight as a powerful affirmation of who they are and what they do, both within and apart from their involvement in the life of their congregation. They come to a deeper realization that God is present and at work in the everyday world, not just in times and activities that seem overtly religious. This realization broadens their perspective. It helps them discover new possibilities for finding meaning and purpose in their lives. It is heartening for them to celebrate the fact that the church of Jesus Christ is not interested in people merely to recruit their talents for more and more congregational activities. Nor does the church want them to scatter into their daily lives solely for the purpose of making converts; that is, recruiting more church members. The Christian faith affirms the importance and recognizes the dignity of the normal daily labors of believers as activities that can express their commitment to Christ as well as serve their God.

God calls Christian men and women to live as people who experience the gracious presence of God in their home and family time, their leisure and recreation activities, their civic and community responsibilities, and the time they spend at work. In this book, I focus primarily on how God's call relates to that portion of a person's life spent going about his or her daily work. Here is an arena that occupies a significant portion of the energies and attentions of most adults. Yet, it is an arena that can seem to have little connection to the faith of the church.

By *daily work*, I mean those purposeful and productive activities to which people devote a great deal of their time and energy on a regular basis week after week, activities that yield a beneficial result for themselves or for those around them. Work may or may not be for pay. It may take place in a group setting or in isolation from others. For some people, this work is performed at home. For others, it occurs in formal places of employment. For those in times of transition, their work may include supplementing their education as they prepare for a new direction in their occupational lives. For still others, their life circumstances may allow them to spend considerable amounts of productive time involved in community volunteer activities.

My hope is to encourage readers to explore the relationship between those things that occupy their energies while they work and what it means for them to believe that, as baptized Christians, they have a vocation, a calling from God not just to "go to church," but also to *be* the church at all times and in all places, including in and through their daily labors. That's an easy statement to make, but often a difficult concept for people to grasp as their own, given the complexity of life in the 21st century and our culture's tendency to divide reality into separate and often unrelated compartments. It is not meaningful to offer simplistic answers to the challenging and frustrating questions that arise when Christians begin to connect faith and work. There is value, however, in urging believers to struggle with the seeming discontinuity between Sunday and Monday from the perspective of their "24/7" identity as children of God who need to return daily to the meaning of their baptisms.

The next chapter offers an overview of the many reasons why the connection between the Christian faith and the activities of daily life and work is not more self-evident to many faithful and committed church members. Some of these reasons are rooted in the way Western society has come to view both the purpose of work and the proper role of religion in a person's life. Others are the result of an institutional church that is often unashamedly focused on itself and its own needs. In other words, this is an issue not just for individual believers who want to deepen the meaning of their faith. It is also an issue for congregations, for the whole Christian community in its quest to be faithful to its calling to proclaim the message that the church is a people.

For reflection

1. When have you had an experience in the workplace that led you to say, "Surely the Lord is in this place"? (Genesis 28:16 NRSV)
2. How much do you know about the daily work of others in your congregation? Find out what fellow members do on a daily basis. Ask what excites them and what frustrates them about their work. Use this information to begin a daily regimen of prayer for them.
3. What do you think about before worship? Be more intentional about reviewing the joys and frustrations of the past week and bringing them to God. What elements of the worship experience stick with you the most as you leave? Be more intentional about letting them inform how you will respond to the joys and frustrations of the coming week.
4. What do you think of when you hear the words "minister" and "priest"? Reflect on the Christian tradition that says these words describe you—whether you are ordained or not, whether you work at a church or not.

2

How the Split Came to Be

Not long ago I started to cry during a sermon and was unable to stay in my pew. The preacher was talking about visiting the offices of his city government; he spoke about how evil that place was, unlike the sacred (sanctuary) space we were inhabiting at that moment. I had to leave because some of the people in that congregation–especially the twenty-somethings–were by that sermon discouraged from even considering a call to work in politics or public service. This was another example of how, in its presentation of the world, the church seems to mitigate against seeing all of life as sacred.[1]

Work is an important part of the self-understanding of most adults. It's how they spend many of their waking hours. One of the first things they ask each other in social settings is, "What do you do?" Where I live, what a person did at work is included in virtually every obituary. Work and worth, job and identity are closely related.

In centuries past, the institutional church played a role in the rhythm of daily work in Western society. The ringing of the church bells summoned people to their labors and announced the end of the working day. No longer does the church have such an overt influence over this important everyday experience.

Today, many people tend to compartmentalize their lives. They keep separate and unrelated the activities they pursue and the relationships they maintain in their places of work, with their families, and at their congregations.

A great many factors contribute to the disconnect between church activity and daily work activity, even among the most committed church members. The purpose of this chapter is to identify a number of these factors. Some are inherent in the way Western culture views both the nature of work and the role of religion. Others are the fault of the church itself.

Because the tendency to separate faith and daily living is so powerful and so prevalent, it might be tempting to lament that little can be done to change it. I believe it is possible, however, for the church to rise to the challenge of assisting its members to be conscious of their Christian identity as an asset for them as they go about their weekday work. Therefore, this chapter will conclude with a vision of how local congregations can be more effective and more proactive in encouraging all the baptized to make the connection between Sunday and Monday, between the faith they profess and the lives they lead at work.

The purpose and meaning of work

First, however, it will be helpful to examine the way in which Western culture has understood the purpose and the meaning of work. Daily labor is a great provider of worth for most adults who hear early in their lives the challenge to "make something of yourself." A person's job title, security, and salary grade are important measures of that person's value in society. *Habits of the Heart*, the landmark treatment of modern individualism, puts it this way: "It is a widely held middle-class—and American—view that through work one gains self-respect and the ability to control, at least in part, one's environment."[2]

This widely held view can create a tremendous sense of frustration and diminished self-esteem for those who are unemployed or underemployed as well as for those who do work for which they are not paid—such as homemakers and students. While in graduate school, I entered a store to purchase a computer. Predictably, the first question the salesperson asked me was, "What do you do?" When he discovered that I was pursuing an advanced degree in historical theology and that I spent my days translating medieval Latin and German manuscripts, his face took on a bemused expression. He shook his head and exclaimed, "Talk about esoteric. That's what I call knowledge for knowledge's sake." That salesperson was so baffled as to why a healthy adult male was not engaged in providing for the needs of his family that it never occurred to him that his insult was depriving him of a commission. I got his message, though, a message I received in many similar incidents: My worth in the eyes of most people was related integrally to the job I held or did not hold.

Interestingly, my wife has experienced similar reactions from acquaintances who could not understand why she would leave her position as a teacher to raise our small children—with a similar stab to her self-esteem. The voices linking *paid* work and worth are loud and clear in our society. No wonder it has been said that for many adults the lack of work is feared just as much as is the diagnosis of a terminal illness.

Why do work and worth seem to be so closely related? Is it because work *per se* is a blessing, an opportunity for people to express their potential? Or is it because work, albeit a curse in and of itself, at least provides them with the means to accumulate the material wealth that is an undisputed symbol of status in our culture?

Historically, Western civilization has had an ambivalent appreciation for the dignity of work. In ancient Greek thought, manual labor in particular was considered degrading. Working was seen merely as a means—an often unpleasant means—to a far greater end. The goal of any refined person was to rise above it, to escape the need for it, and to spend one's time in contemplation. The classical understanding of work, reinforced by the image in Genesis

3:19 of labor as a curse associated with the fall of humanity, played a role in the medieval church's elevation of the contemplative life.

This image also makes sense to laborers in our contemporary industrial and postindustrial world whose tasks are often so uncreative and monotonous it is difficult to see them as anything more than necessary evils to be endured in order to secure a paycheck. There is often little sense of personal contribution or "craftsmanship" on an assembly line or in a maze of office cubicles. No wonder many employees dream of being able to escape the routine of daily work. Their ultimate goal, to be sure, is no longer a life of contemplation. Rather, it is one of leisure.

On the other hand, there are people who recognize in the tasks of their daily work an opportunity to express themselves, to utilize their gifts, and to experience the invigoration that comes from meeting and overcoming challenges. They are honored to identify themselves by the work they do. In fact, work can become for them such a source of well-being that they spend increasing amounts of time in their labors, neglecting family relationships, civic responsibilities, and the need for rest and leisure. This is the contemporary phenomenon of the *workaholic*. These are people who let their occupations become almost the sole focus of their interests and their energies— not because they want a larger paycheck, but because it is at work that they feel best about themselves. Woe to them if they are faced with retirement or job loss. Such a change can deflate or destroy their understanding of their personal significance.

Both of the above attitudes toward work are aberrations that sap the joy from the rhythm of daily living. I have read a wide variety of assessments regarding how satisfied contemporary workers are with their jobs. Depending on whom you believe, anywhere between 29% and 95% of America's working population do not enjoy the work they do. Even the low-end estimate represents a significant number of people. Church members are not immune to the love-hate or hate-hate relationship that many people have with their daily work.

For this reason, since the mid-20th century there have been voices urging the church to articulate a clearer theology of work, one that wrestles with the ambivalent view of work that is present in scripture no less than in classical thought. The Bible in many places affirms the positive value of work. Even before the fall, humanity is given work to do (Genesis 1:28; 2:15). God is the primary worker and one aspect of being made in God's image is humanity's ability to join its maker in productive activity. Yet, Genesis 3 does make "the sweat of your face" sound much more like a curse (Genesis 3:17-19; see also Genesis 5:29).

In the gospels, Jesus spends much of his time among people in their places of work and often uses workday imagery in his teachings and parables. The New Testament letters encourage members of the fledgling Christian community to be industrious (2 Thessalonians 3:6, 7, 11; 1 Timothy 5:13). Yet, the New Testament also teaches there are limits to the value of our daily labor (Luke 12:16-21). None of our work can bring us closer to God.

Pondering this ambivalent understanding of work in scripture and Western history, contemporary believers can both affirm its positive value and be wary of its limits. Through their productivity they can honor the one who made them. At the same time, they must be on their guard to avoid the many ways their jobs threaten to possess and enslave them.

Societal factors

The above comments suggest that there is value in examining the meaning and purpose of work from a broader perspective, particularly from the perspective of faith in God and the conviction of God's gracious activity in the world. Yet, that is something that most workers, even most devoted Christian workers, never think to do. There are a number of reasons for this. This section explores some of the societal and cultural factors that mitigate against relating faith and daily work.

1. In the fragmentation of realities that characterizes life for many in our society, religion, along with home and family, is often considered a part of one's private life, divorced from the public world of work. It is not that people choose not to relate Sunday and Monday, faith and work. It is just that the notion seldom occurs to them. This tendency toward the privatization of religion weakens its capacity to be a transforming agency in society. *Habits of the Heart* explains it this way:

> Privatization placed religion, together with the family, in a compartmentalized sphere that provided loving support but could no longer challenge the dominance of utilitarian values in the society at large. Indeed, to the extent that privatization succeeded, religion was in danger of becoming, like the family, "a haven in a heartless world," but one that did more to reinforce that world, by caring for its casualties, than to challenge its assumptions.[3]

2. A second phenomenon that tends to dissolve the relationship between faith and daily work is the pluralistic nature of contemporary society. Whether out of respect for the differing views of fellow workers, a desire to avoid the kind of tension produced when people disagree regarding things about which they have strong feelings, or a cynicism born of wondering whether any of the competing religious worldviews is correct, people in a pluralistic work environment tend to keep their faith to themselves. This attitude is evidenced in such frequently heard comments as: "My faith is between me and God" and "What I believe is my own business." It is a short step from the tacit taboo on speaking

about one's faith at work to seldom giving any thought to how one's faith is related to that work and workplace. To the extent that any religious sentiments are expressed in the public arena of daily work today, they have little more content than a bland moral code of honesty, fairness, and leading a good life—what is often referred to as "civil religion."

3. There is also a practical issue. Many people today commute long distances from the pristine surroundings in which their homes and congregations may be set to the more hectic and cosmopolitan surroundings of their workplaces. The change in geography may not seem significant, but psychologically this does make it easier to separate the issues and concerns of one location from those of the other.

4. The complexity and rapid pace of work plays a role in the Sunday–Monday split. The workplace can be so highly technological, impersonal, and fast-paced that it affords little time and no encouragement to pause for periods of reflection on the deeper meaning and implications, if any, of one's tasks. For example, it is easier to keep separate in one's thinking Sunday's emphasis on grace and Monday's emphasis on productivity than it is to figure out what meaning the central affirmation of the Christian faith has in an achievement-oriented workplace.

5. The materialism that drives so much of late 20th and early 21st century life also serves to discourage faith-based workplace reflection. Many adults find their labors motivated by a desire to accumulate goods for themselves, rather than to contribute to the good of the world around them. This motivation is learned and reinforced early. I cannot recall when I have heard a teenager speak about career hopes in terms of the service he or she might perform. Typically, comments center around the salary the young person hopes to make. In *Habits of the Heart*, the views of one

interviewee led the researchers to conclude: "The person who thinks in terms of the common good is a 'sucker' in a situation where each individual is trying to pursue his or her own interests."[4]

These five societal realities reinforce the tendency of workers to disassociate the faith they profess from the conduct of their daily work. They represent attitudes toward work, life, and faith that are pervasive and deeply rooted. It is not likely that the Christian community will be able to alter these realities significantly. The church should, however, be aware of them and support believers in efforts to resist subscribing to them blindly.

The church's complicity

Instead, the institutional church itself often stands in the way of people making this connection between the faith they hold and the work they do. In *All God's People Are Ministers,* Patricia Page quotes the comments of a woman who is "director of compensation research" for a major bank:

> My church does not seem to know much about. . .my work. I would like to see the churches relating more to the strengths and opportunities of their business members, to their areas where they excel, rather than waiting as it were until they lose their jobs, and then moving in to comfort and counsel with them.[5]

The institutional church is guilty not only of failing to aid its members in relating faith and life. It is not too strong to say that the church as an organization is sometimes actively involved in discouraging them from making such a connection. Celia Hahn writes in her article, "Where in the World Is the Church?": "The ecclesiastical universe acknowledges only church work. As one laywoman put it, 'the Church has only been interested in, and supportive of, the work I do *at* and *for* the Church.'"[6]

It is the nature of institutions to be inward centered, focused on issues of self-preservation—maintenance and survival. Interestingly, being "curved inward" is a traditional definition for sin. Sin and its debilitating consequences affect institutions as well as individuals. The church is not immune to this tendency.

The clergy especially are susceptible to focusing almost exclusively on the organizational needs of the church, assuming that these are more important than anything else. For most pastors, the church as institution is their weekday world, their workplace. Its needs are for them matters of daily concern. At the same time, they may understand very little about what interests and challenges those who work outside the organization of the church.

In its theology, the Christian church is clear that its organizational structures were never intended to be ends in themselves. They are instruments for assisting members in the mission to *bring* the good news and *be* the good news of God's amazing love and gracious acceptance wherever they are, through whatever they do; that is, to relate their faith to every aspect of their lives. Why is it, then, that the operational message of the church differs so greatly from its formal message? Why do church leaders spend so much energy on in-house concerns and so little on sending members out to be God's people in the world? Why is it so difficult for the church, by the power of the Holy Spirit, to rise above institutional inertia?

One factor lies in the history of how lay people have been valued in the church. The next chapter will review the development of a two-tiered Christianity, in which bishops, pastors, and other members of the church's ordained leadership were perceived to be more important than the average Christian lay person. By the late Middle Ages, a guiding assumption in the church was that the responsibilities of lay people were to come to the institution and support the institution (i.e., pray and pay). There was little sense that the institution of the church had a responsibility to help lay people go into daily life with the tools to express their faith in reflected and intentional ways. Remnants of a two-tiered Christianity are still in evidence today. The common understanding of the term "lay person"—referring to someone who is uninformed, a follower who needs the guidance of a professional—reflects this assumption.

By contrast, pastors enjoy an elevated status in the minds of many church members. They are treated with deference. The tacit assumption is that they are somehow holier, closer to God. The congregation I serve recently called a seminary graduate to serve as assistant pastor. She was unprepared for how differently people, even long-time acquaintances, began to act around her following her ordination. Such treatment can be seductive.

It is tempting for pastors to reinforce the traditional distinction between clergy and laity. It is also tempting for lay people to accept the distinction, since it frees them from certain responsibilities. For example: "The pastor ought to be the one to pray before our meetings. That's what she's paid for." Or, "How can you expect me to figure out how my faith relates to my work? I'm just a lay person."

Another reason why many committed Christians, lay and ordained, do not resist the institutional tendency to focus the energies of church members inward is the genuine and pressing organizational needs of the church. The efforts of many committed workers, paid and volunteer, are needed if congregations are to maintain their worship, educational, and caring ministries. These ministries serve the needs of people both within the church and in the larger community. Through them the gospel is proclaimed in word and deed. I do not wish to devalue the importance of such church-sponsored activities. Rather, I lament the tunnel vision that promotes these activities alone as vital ministries and does not balance a call for believers to put their faith into action by "getting involved at church" with a reminder that faith can also be put into action in the ordinary activities of a person's daily routine.

A third reason why pastors and other congregational leaders do not work harder to counteract the inward orientation of the church as institution stems from their own participation in the value system of the larger culture in which they live. Church professionals like to feel successful in what they do. Many, in spite of the Christian ideal of servanthood, have aspirations of rising to larger and more prestigious positions. How is their success measured? What criteria are used when deciding who advances and who does not? In "The Sunday-Monday Gap," Edward White writes:

> Most denominations require their congregations to compile an annual statistical report. The form does not normally ask whether lives are being transformed or people are discovering their call to ministry in daily life. The form asks, "How many bucks, bodies, and buildings has your congregation generated this year?"
>
> Pretty soon the preacher gets the message. What really counts in the church is not the ministry of Word and Sacrament, but the generation of positive statistics. The clergy are evaluated according to those numbers, and that is what they are rewarded for, usually with a call to a larger congregation with a bigger salary. Caring about the quality and faithfulness of the lives of church members generally is not rewarded.[7]

Obviously, it is difficult for church leaders to proclaim, "The Gospel compels all the baptized to go out and live the transforming power of God's grace in the things they do day-by-day," when for so many reasons those same leaders are preoccupied with involving people in more and more in-house activities. In *The Monday Connection*, William Diehl describes his impression of this discontinuity:

> The gap between the rhetoric of what the church was saying on Sunday and the reality of what was happening in my life on Monday was enormous. The problem was that my church was speaking as an

extrovert, but behaving as an introvert. It was calling on me to serve as a disciple of Christ in the world without giving me any help on how to do it. On the other hand, I got help in the form of affirmation, training, and even prayers for my service in the church as a Sunday school teacher, youth advisor, and church council member. For my Monday work as a Christian businessperson in a highly competitive environment, however, I received no affirmation, no training, no support, no prayers. Nothing. There was absolutely no connection between Sunday and Monday.[8]

Diehl suggests four ways in which the church's words and actions do not correlate: in its affirmations, its training, its support, and its corporate prayer. Let's examine them in reverse order:

1. *For what and for whom does the church pray?* Typically in Sunday worship, prayers are offered for the ministries of the congregation and church-at-large, for governmental leaders, for the sick and needy, the dying and grieving, and others in crisis situations. Occasionally petitions will be offered for students and teachers (at the beginning of a school year), or for health-care workers (in the context of caring for the sick), or for parents (on Mother's and Father's Days). Seldom will there be any mention of those who spend forty hours or more a week in offices or factory floors or other places of work.

2. *For whom does the church offer support ministries?* It is typically for those in a common stage of life—like young mothers, singles, or senior citizens, or those going through times of extraordinary difficulty—recovering alcoholics, those grieving the loss of loved ones, cancer sufferers, and the like. Jacqueline McMakin and Rhoda Nary write:

What is often neglected is the support of people who are not in crisis—the many people in fairly stable situations who yearn to make their lives count, to contribute meaningfully to society, to do their part in embodying Gospel values.[9]

Few congregations offer any vehicle that focuses on providing encouragement or support for members as they endeavor to relate the charge to "live faithfully" with fulfilling the concrete obligations of their daily work.

3. *For whom does the church offer training?* Many congregations offer orientation sessions for newly elected members of their governing board. The regional judicatory of which my congregation is a member holds annual workshops for congregational presidents, Sunday school teachers, youth leaders, and committee members. On the other hand, one seldom hears of church-sponsored courses revolving around "how to make your faith an asset at work" or "how to live more intentionally as a Christian day-by-day." No wonder many Christians identify their duties as faithful followers of Christ largely in terms of the things they do "at church."

4. *Whom does the church recognize and honor?* Shortly after Labor Day, many congregations hold services of installation—in the context of Sunday worship—for their Sunday school teachers. Teachers are asked to stand before the gathered assembly. They are told how much their commitment to teach is valued. Other church members are asked to support the teachers through their prayers. Similar rites honor officers of the congregation. At the 2001 assembly of the Northeastern Pennsylvania Synod of the ELCA, I had the privilege of presiding over a commissioning service aimed at affirming all those present in their efforts to live faithfully in concrete ways every day—at home, work, school, wherever they find themselves. Afterward, many people commented on the power of the experience, a power accentuated by the fact that none of them had ever experienced anything similar in all their years as committed members of the church. They were

more accustomed to having their congregations make them feel guilty because they are not doing more at church.

When church members are prayed for, supported, trained, and affirmed for the things they are doing in daily life and work, quite often they experience the unexpected affirmation as tremendously liberating and empowering. I have heard them exclaim, "You mean I'm doing it?! You mean I *am* expressing my commitment to Christ in and through the things I do each day?"

Pastors obviously play a key role in helping believers connect faith and life, church and world. Unfortunately, pastors are often poorly informed about what the members of their congregations do in daily life. They know who teaches Sunday school, who is willing to cut the church lawn, and who is comfortable reading the lessons at worship, but they may not know where people work, what their jobs entail, or how secure their employment situations are. Most pastors have little sense of what questions lay people are asking or what struggles and challenges they face.

When pastors do speak about daily work in sermons, their comments often are simplistic. Not knowing what to say about the will of God for people in their work, clergy often focus on the message that God wants people to be fulfilled by what they do. They think they are proclaiming good news. For those who are in positions that offer little sense of fulfillment, however, such comments simply add one more burden to the person's life. "Great! God wants me to be happy in my work. I can't even do that right."

It is not unusual for illustrations about daily work in sermons to be negative. The reflection piece by Sally Simmel with which this chapter begins notes how one pastor warned against the godlessness of the civic arena. In a similar way, the world of business is often excoriated for its competitiveness and materialism. It is important to reflect on competition and materialism (and godlessness) in the context of the Christian faith. But church members live in the material world and deal with issues of competition—healthy and unhealthy—on a daily basis. No one likes to hear blanket condemnations of the activities they pursue for most of their waking hours, in places where they have made friends and experienced satisfactions.

Worse, many pastors are unaware of how little they understand the working lives of their parishioners. They are convinced that in their preaching and teaching they truly are helping people make meaningful faith and life connections.

Certainly, parish pastors cannot experience personally the working conditions that each day drain or exhilarate congregational members who engage in a wide variety of occupations and are scattered in many places of employment. Few pastors are experts on labor or business or the challenges of homemaking. Most people don't expect them to be. But pastors can ask members what their work is like. They can honor members by visiting them in the workplace and taking an interest in what occupies so much of their time. They can stop talking about doctrine and the latest trends in this or that area of congregational ministry long enough to listen to the joys and concerns people encounter Monday through Saturday. In that way they can move closer to being able to speak God's word in ways that will make sense to people who spend so much of their lives in the world of work.

A new vision for the church

Half a century ago, Elton Trueblood declared:

> The modern church will not make a sufficient difference by a slight improvement in the anthems or by a little better preaching or by a little better organization of the Sunday Schools. . . . What we need is a radical change of some kind.[10]

Trueblood called this radical change, "lay religion." There are many indications that such a new and radical vision for the church is still needed.

In this new vision of the church, by the grace of God, God's people will grow to understand their daily tasks as having meaning and value beyond their role in securing a paycheck, even if these tasks are not the source of all meaning. They will hear the message that their labors are good, even if they are not ends in themselves. They will be more conscious of the Christian affirmation that they are God's co-workers. They will embrace a perspective from which they can critique surrounding culture, even though they are not removed from it.

In this new vision of the church, leaders will not co-opt all of the energies of congregational members for in-house activities. The leader's role will be to encourage the baptized to search for the connections between faith and work—listening to their struggles, affirming them for their faithfulness, and working with them to develop more effective tools for bringing their Christianity to life every day of the week. The leaders will reject the mindset that suggests the only measure of a person's commitment is the amount of time he or she spends involved in the activities of the institution. They will have high expectations of congregational members—expectations not only about the kind of difference the members can make around the parish, but even more about the kind of difference each member can make in the world. They will appreciate lay people as the front-line troops in God's mission and themselves as the behind the scenes supporters.

Pastors will need to teach more effectively the rhythm of gathering and scattering that is meant to govern the Christian's life, reminding all that the purpose of the gathering times is to prepare for and reflect upon the experiences of daily living. They will urge church members to examine their attitudes toward life and work critically, in light of their faith, and to evaluate prevailing cultural assumptions in the context of Christian teaching. This will not take place in a heavy-handed way, but will begin where the people are—acknowledging the complexity of the real-life issues with which they struggle. The local congregation will no longer be the place to which people come for all the answers. Rather it will be a safe place in which to raise and ponder difficult questions.

The urgency to turn this new vision into a reality has seldom been greater. Traditional securities are breaking down in our society. Life at work is far more varied and complex than ever. People are asking questions such as, "Where do I find significance in my life?" "Whatever happened to loyalty from employers?" "Who appreciates what I do?"

Traditional understandings of the church and its role in society are also breaking down. People are looking for more from their congregations than busy places with lots of programs. They are longing for their church and its leaders to proclaim the old, old story of Jesus and his love in ways that speak to the concerns, opportunities, and frustrations of daily living.

One tool at the church's disposal for assisting Christian lay people and clergy in talking about the difficult issues of relating faith and work is the teaching on vocation, as articulated by Martin Luther and other reformers in the 16th century. The affirmation that God's call comes to all the baptized in the context of all their experiences provides a framework to help believers focus their thinking about how Sunday relates to Monday. It is rooted in the confidence that God, the Creator, is still at work in and through the structures of daily life. It encourages workers to notice how their activities benefit their neighbors and thereby have value in the eyes of God. It endeavors to overcome the gulf between the sacred and the secular by understanding all of life as an expression of faith.

The next chapter examines Martin Luther's teaching on vocation in detail and notes the power it had in his generation for helping Christians listen for God's call to them. The remaining chapters will address the question, "Can the teaching on vocation have such power for Christians today?"

For reflection

1. Ponder the comment that many people tend to compartmentalize their lives. To what extent is this true for you? What is lost when faith is separated from daily routine?
2. What is your daily work? What elements of your day seem like a blessing? What elements seem like a curse? What are the connection points between your identity as a worker and your identity as a child of God?
3. What interferes with your ability to hear God's call to you in daily life? What might help you become a better listener?
4. If you are a pastor or congregational leader, how have you been affected by the temptation to be "inward centered," thinking mainly about what members can do for the organization of the church? What can you do to change your focus?

3

A Resource from Our Heritage

So you might say, "How then if I am not called. What shall I do then?" Answer: How is it possible that you should not be called? You will always be in a station. You are either a husband or wife or son or daughter or male or female servant . . . See, since now no one is without some command and calling, so no one is without some kind of work, if he or she desires to do right. All, therefore, are to take heed to remain in their calling, look to themselves, do faithfully what they are commanded and serve God, keeping God's laws.[1]

Jürgen Moltmann, reflecting on the relationship of theology and ethics, the correlation between Christian doctrine and faithful Christian living, comments: "Next to Word and Sacrament, the recognition of the divine vocation of every Christian in his or her worldly occupation is the third great insight of the Lutheran Reformation."[2] As Martin Luther's evangelical theology developed in response to what he perceived as a "Babylonian captivity" of the people of God by an oppressive and elitist ecclesiastical hierarchy, one of its key assertions was that every baptized person has a calling from God. Each child of God is given the responsibility and the opportunity to live in response to God's saving activity in Jesus Christ. This vocation of the Christian plays a role in the whole life of a person. It gives purpose and meaning to all of his or her activities and relationships. It also reveals the limits of those activities and relationships. None are ends in themselves—except the relationship with God, whom believers are called to glorify in all that they say and do. Luther in no way restricted the notion of a divine vocation to the occupational life of the Christian, but certainly his teaching on the subject came to play an important role in the way in which his followers understood the meaning of their daily work.

Vocation in Christian history

Since this teaching, like much of Martin Luther's theology, was formed in a polemical context; that is, in passionate response to what he considered to be a distortion of authentic Christian tradition, it is helpful to begin with a brief review of the church's use of the term vocation from its biblical roots until the beginning of the 16th century. *Vocatio* is the Latin equivalent of the Hebrew word *Qara'* and Greek *klésis*. Each of these words can be translated "calling."

In the Hebrew scriptures, *Qara'* most often is a general term meaning: to announce or name or summon. It describes God's invitation to enter into an intimate relationship with God (Psalm 41:2; Isaiah 43:1, 45:3, 49:1). When God calls specific individuals to specific tasks, it is typically for the good of the entire community (Exodus 3:1-15, 19:3). God calls the chosen people to participate in God's grand purpose for the world. They are to be God's agents who will enlighten all the inhabitants of the world (Isaiah 42:6). They are summoned to service, not to greatness.

Similarly, in the New Testament, *klésis* typically refers to the invitation for individuals to experience a relationship with God and God's people (Romans 1:6-7; 1 Corinthians 1:9; 1 Peter 2:9). The appropriate response to God's call is faith in Jesus Christ, faith expressed actively as discipleship or obedience. The power of this call is rooted in the creative word of God—God's ability to call things into being (Romans 4:17). Those who are saved are gathered together in a community of the called, the *ekklésia*.

In other words, all Christians are called by God (Acts 2:39; Romans 1:6). All receive God's promises. To all gifts have been given. From all obedience is expected. All have a vocation to serve God and others in their daily lives (Ephesians 4:1-13). The Bible does not divide God's people into classes—such as lay and clergy. All believers are *called to be*, to be holy (1 Peter 1:15). And they are *called to do*, to do God's will (1 Thessalonians 2:12). All God's people are given the honor of participating in God's work. They are not called out of the world so much as called to serve God in the world. As is true in the Hebrew scriptures, calling has to do with service, not status (Galatians 5:13; 1 Peter 3:9).

One New Testament passage bears special mention in light of the importance Martin Luther placed on it in his development of the evangelical doctrine of vocation: 1 Corinthians 7:20-24.

Let each of you remain in the condition [klésis] in which you were called. Were you a slave when called? Do not be concerned about it. Even if you can gain your freedom, make use of your present condition now more than ever. For whoever was called in the Lord as a slave is a freed person belonging to the Lord, just as whoever was free when called is a slave of Christ. You were bought with a price; do not become slaves of human masters. In whatever condition you were called, brothers and sisters, there remain with God.

Paul may be suggesting merely that it is not worth the trouble of changing one's life situation in light of the imminent return of Christ, but the above verses also remind readers that God's call comes to each person within the context of his or her unique setting. Living a life of service to God does not require a change of outward circumstances, of social or occupational status. People can respond to God's call where they are.

Martin Luther found such an affirmation to have great meaning. It seemed to him that Paul had made a bold declaration that

God is concerned with the daily activities of Christian men and women and that God calls them to responsible discipleship within the performance of those daily activities.

In the first hundred and fifty years after Christ, Christian writers echoed the witness of scripture that the call of God is primarily a synonym for God's saving action in Christ. It comes to all the baptized. It gives each believer a vocation, the charge to live in gratitude to God and service to others. At this time, there was no firm and consistent division of Christians into a higher order of clergy who possess a special calling and the general order of laity who are merely the supporters and the recipients of the clergy's ministry.

By the 3rd century, however, this began to change. As the church grew, it accrued more institutional elements. Formal offices replaced an earlier charismatic leadership. There was a growing sense in the church that the clergy were called to a higher dignity by virtue of their office. Under Constantine, in the 4th century, members of the clergy were accorded privileges previously granted to the heathen priesthood.

With the rise of monasticism, vocation became associated with the summons to a lifestyle of acetic simplicity. Most Christians, engaged in the daily struggle of maintaining a household and raising a family, could not devote themselves to what were supposed to be more God-pleasing religious pursuits. Thomas Aquinas and other Medieval theologians carried this mindset further, disparaging manual work as evidence of God's punishment of a fallen humanity, useful only to the extent that it teaches workers discipline.

By the 12th century, this gradual, but persistent elevation of church office holders as those possessing a higher calling, nobler form of work, and closer relationship with God was complete. Gratiani, a canon lawyer, wrote in his Decretals: "There are two kinds of Christians: the kind that possess a divine office and are given to contemplation and prayer, who agree to desist from all temporal clatter. These are the clergy who are devoted to God . . . . And the other kind of Christians who are the laity."[3]

More and more the lives of those in holy orders were spent in contemplation, pilgrimages, and other (from the point of view of Luther) self-focused, rather than neighbor-focused pursuits. More and more, those who held official positions in the church enjoyed their elevated status and gave little thought to the servant character of their roles.

Martin Luther on vocation

It was in reaction to this mindset that Martin Luther developed his teaching on vocation. In so doing, he discarded violently the technical meaning it had come to have in medieval Roman Catholic theology, designating a special, elevated status for those in holy orders. Instead Luther elaborated on an idea already espoused by certain 14th and 15th century mystics that the call of God was meant for the humblest laborer as well as for priests and bishops, monks and nuns.

Martin Luther's bold claim was that all the tasks of one's life, any Christian's life, no matter how menial or mundane the tasks performed, provide an opportunity to express one's faith. For Luther, vocation was not a call to abandon the nitty-gritty of the world for a more pious and more prestigious status. Rather it was a calling to and within the place where one carries out one's everyday labors. There is an honorable character to the ordinary acts Christian men and women perform as they engage in the responsibilities of their various occupations. These responsibilities are honorable simply because they enhance the lives of individuals or the community and thereby contribute to God's good intentions for humanity. In this way, Luther breached the boundary between what the medieval church celebrated as sacred and what it dismissed as merely secular.

In medieval theology, the sacrament of ordination divided Christianity into two levels of status. Martin Luther focused instead on the Sacrament of Holy Baptism as the sign of God's call to all Christians, giving them an identity from which Christian living flows. In a sermon from 1534, he wrote:

> See to it first of all that you believe in Christ and are baptized. Afterward, see to your vocation. I am called to be a preacher. Now when I preach I perform a holy work that is pleasing to God. If you are a father or mother, believe in Jesus Christ and so you will be a holy father and a holy mother. Pay attention to the early years of your children, let them pray, and discipline and spank them. Oversee the running of the household and the preparation of meals. These things are none other than holy works to which you have been called. That means they are your holy life and are a part of God's Word and your vocation.[4]

Luther's exegetical writings provided a frequent medium for articulating his teaching about the vocation and the dignity of every Christian engaged in the pursuit of his or her daily labors. What follows is a portion of his lectures on Genesis 17:9, in which God says to Abraham, "You shall keep my covenant":

> Every person surely has a calling. While attending to it he serves God. A king serves God when he is at pains to look after and govern his people. So do the mother of a household when she tends her baby, the father of a household when he gains a livelihood by working, and a pupil when he applies himself diligently to his studies. . . . Therefore, it is a great wisdom when a human being does what God commands and earnestly devotes himself to his vocation without taking into consideration what others are doing.[5]

Like so much of his theology, the teaching on vocation grew out of Martin Luther's understanding of the justification of the Christian by grace through faith. It is through God's initiative and saving activity in Jesus Christ that individuals find their Christian identity. They need do nothing to work themselves toward a salutary relationship with God. God has already offered such a relationship without human effort or cooperation. Instead, believers can approach their daily tasks as opportunities to respond to God in faith and thanksgiving.

They do this, in particular, by serving God's children, their fellow human beings. This is what Luther expressed in the thesis statement of his treatise, *On the Freedom of the Christian*: "A Christian is a perfectly free lord of all, subject to none. A Christian is a perfectly dutiful servant of all, subject to all."[6] Freed by Christ from the need to earn God's favor through requirements and rituals, God's people can turn their attentions to caring for others through the use of their everyday gifts and in the performance of their everyday activities. As sinners, people may experience their secular occupations in a negative way—as menial drudgery—as did the medieval monastic tradition against which Luther was reacting. As justified sinners, in relationship with a gracious God, they can see these same occupations as avenues for expressing their vocation to give glory to God as they address the needs of God's people.

Martin Luther's vocation teaching is related to his often quoted insight that all the baptized are part of a universal priesthood of believers. This notion, too, Luther developed in response to the arrogance of the ecclesiastical hierarchy of his day. He affirmed the dignity of every Christian as a valued servant of God. In "To the Christian Nobility of the German Nation," he wrote:

It is a pure invention that pope, bishop, priests, and monks are called the spiritual estate while princes, lords, artisans, and farmers are called the temporal estate. This is indeed a piece of deceit and hypocrisy. Yet no one is intimidated by it, and for this reason: all Christians are truly of the spiritual estate, and there is no difference among them except that of office. . . . We are all consecrated priests through baptism.[7]

Luther's use of vocation and universal priesthood differ primarily in terms of what each invites the faithful recipient of God's grace to do. That all Christians are priests means that they all (not just those who hold formal offices in the church) have the privilege and the responsibility to declare to their neighbors the good news of God's redeeming grace. That all Christians have a vocation means that they are to render service to their neighbors simply through the performance of their useful daily tasks.

The key commonality between Martin Luther's insight regarding the universal priesthood of believers and his teaching on vocation was his insistence that at the heart of a person's response to God should be an overwhelming desire to love and serve his or her neighbors. What makes work God-pleasing and valuable is that it is community oriented. Relationship with God moves people to redirect their inherently self-centered focus away from themselves toward Christ who alone can save and toward their neighbors through whom Christ is present among them.

If you are a manual laborer, you find that the Bible has been put into your workshop, into your hand, into your heart. It teaches and preaches how you should treat your neighbor. Just look at your tools—at your needle or thimble, your beer barrel, your goods, your scales or yardsticks or measure—and you will read this statement inscribed on them. Everywhere you look, it stares at you. Nothing that you handle every day is so tiny that it does not continually tell you this, if you will only listen. Indeed, there is no shortage of preaching. You have as many preachers as you have transactions, goods, tools, and other equipment in your house and home. All this is continually crying out to you: "Friend, use me in your relations with your neighbor just as you would want your neighbor to use his property in his relations with you."[8]

The great flaw of the medieval monastic system, according to Luther, was that it limited service to God to "religious" acts—the saying of private masses, the making of pilgrimages, and a withdrawal from the mundane activities of the world. It angered Luther that for all their piety, monks and nuns were essentially useless to society around them. The so-called "menial" tasks of householders and laborers contributed far more tangibly to the needs of other people. Luther wrote: "Hence when a maid milks the cows or a hired man hoes the field—provided that they are believers, namely that they conclude that this kind of life is pleasing to God and was instituted by God—they serve God more than all the monks and nuns."[9]

Luther wrote positively about any form of work that was not inherently dishonest or destructive to society. "Every occupation has its own honor before God, as well as its own requirements or duties. . . . God is a great lord and has many kinds of servants."[10] This conviction allowed Luther to extol the labors not only of people from every strata of society, but also of people of both genders. He heralded the daily work of women as being far more acceptable to God than the oft-praised tasks of the clerics. In his explanation of the Ten Commandments in *The Large Catechism*, he wrote:

> If this could be impressed on the poor people, a servant girl would dance for joy and praise and thank God; and with her careful work, for which she receives sustenance and wages, she would obtain a treasure such as those who are regarded as the greatest saints do not have. Is it not a tremendous honor to know this and say, "If you do your

daily household chores, that is better than the holiness and austere life of all the monks?"[11]

Ordinary daily work is holy because it is anchored in faith in Christ, even though it is performed by sinful women and men. It does not bring a person to God, but flows from the new life God in Christ has already given her or him. The content of the work is not as important as the spirit in which it is done.

> God gives us grace not so that we can walk all over it as the world does, but because God takes an interest in all that we do to our neighbors, good and bad, as though we were doing it to God. If only everyone would regard their service to their neighbors as service to God, the whole world would be filled with *Gottesdienst* ["God-service," the German word for worship]. A servant in the stable, a maid in the kitchen, a child in school—these are merely God's workers and God's servants, if they with diligence do what their father and mother, or the lord and lady of the household gives them to do. Thus would every house be filled with *Gottesdienst*, indeed every house would be a true church in which nothing other than pure *Gottesdienst* was practiced.[12]

The grace of God calls Christians into the reign of God and into new life in Jesus Christ. It does not, however, call them away from life in this world. Christians still live in the world. God is still the world's creator. Through Christ, God's reign is in the world.

Martin Luther's teaching on vocation is closely related to three aspects of his understanding of creation. First, creation is good. Since God commissioned human beings to work already in the story of creation (Genesis 1:28), work must also be good. Second, creation is an on-going reality. God not only made the world "in the beginning." God continues the work of creation day-by-day. God is thoroughly alive in the world. Third, God's present-day work in creation happens through tangible means. God uses the actions of people to care for the earth and provide for the needs of its inhabitants. Commenting on Genesis 31:3, Luther wrote:

> God's people please God even in the least and most trifling matters. For He will be working all things through you; He will milk the cow through you and perform the most servile duties through you, and all the greatest and least duties alike will be pleasing to Him.[13]

The Large Catechism's explanation of the first commandment contains the same thought: "Creatures are only the hands, channels, and means through which God bestows all blessings."[14]

Believers serve God as agents of God's continuous creative activity. "Thus," Luther proclaimed, "through faith a Christian becomes a creator."[15] Notice, it is not to special religious acts that people are called, but to an appreciation of the fact that their normal, everyday acts are means through which God is at work.

From the beginning, God ordained certain "orders of creation"—household (and by extension economic life), government, and the church. In his lectures on Genesis, Luther wrote:

> This life is profitably divided into three orders: (1) life in the home; (2) life in the state; (3) life in the church. To whatever order you belong—whether you are a husband, an officer of the state, or a teacher of the church—look about you, and see whether you have done full justice to your calling."[16]

God gives these orders for the sake of stability in society. All human activity takes place within them. One's roles (each person has several—church member, parent, child, worker) within the orders are his or her "stations," "estates," or "walks of life" (German: *Stände*). These are the contexts in which Christians glorify God through service to their neighbors. At times, Luther used the terms station and vocation as synonyms.

The role of pastors is to inform and instruct "the various estates on how they are to conduct themselves outwardly in their several offices and estates so that they may do what is right in the sight of God."[17] No walk of life is inherently better than any other. Luther wrote: "All estates and works of God are to be praised as highly as they can be and none despised in favor of another."[18]

For this reason Luther encouraged Christians to remain in their present life situations. He wrote:

> There are very few who live satisfied with their lot. The layman longs for the life of a cleric, the pupil wishes to be a teacher, the citizen wants to be a councilor, and each of us loathes his own calling, although there is no other way of serving God than to walk in simple faith and then to stick diligently to one's calling and to keep a good conscience.[19]

It is not that Luther was opposed to social mobility. In fact, one of his reasons for encouraging children from all social strata to receive an education was so that they might have the tools to move into whatever walk of life fit their particular gifts from God. Luther himself experienced the benefits of being able to change his station in order to fulfill his understanding of God's will for his life—from the son of a miner to law student to preacher and professor.

Rather, Luther wanted to be clear that leaving one's present station is not necessary in order to please God. God, "does not want people to change or abandon their vocations, as under the papacy it was once considered piety to have given up one's customary way of life and to have withdrawn into a monastery."[20] He was not saying, "you must stay where you are," so much as "you may stay where you are" and still serve God. In other words, one does not need to escape the routine of daily living in order to be pious. After all, no walk of life plays a role in earning God's favor.

Luther related his teaching on vocation to his understanding of God's law. Stations and vocations are the arenas wherein Christians can discern how to live according to God's commands. The law keeps believers mindful of their sin and reminds them of their obligations. It urges them to realize their fullest potential, even while cautioning them that their work is never an end in itself, since it cannot bring them to God. In this way, the law is not an oppressive burden, but a helpful guide. The law also serves God's purpose of redemption by confronting believers with their inherent tendency to focus their attentions on themselves rather than their neighbors—thereby reminding them of their need for Christ.

Thus, vocation and daily labor are forms of discipline, teaching Christians that although they have been made new in Christ, the old person still remains. This keeps the most loving and neighbor-serving actions in perspective. Such actions, though pleasing to God and used by God, are never perfect. They cannot usher in the kingdom.

Luther knew, of course, that work has its share of frustrations. In a sermon on The Sermon on the Mount, he wrote:

> Love the Word of God and do what is required of you in your station. Then you will experience, both from your neighbors and in your own household, that things will not go as you might wish. You will be hindered and hemmed in on every side, so that you will suffer enough and see enough to make your heart sad.[21]

These frustrations encourage Christians to find refuge and perspective in their faith, in word and sacrament, in God's offer of grace and new beginning. The gospel and the ministry of the church help believers make better sense of the failures and frustrations, the conflicts and even the tragedies they sometimes encounter in the course of their daily labors.

At the same time, the activities of the believer within his or her station are not performed merely out of duty. Christians are *simul iustus et peccator*—saint and sinner at the same time. The old creature must be commanded to follow his or her vocation, but the new creature approaches the same responsibilities willingly and gladly. The obligations of one's station can become labors of spontaneous love, as the love of God graciously given in baptism urges the Christian to loving actions within his or her worldly roles.

Faith stands at the boundary between the two realms—the two ways in which God works in the world, through law and gospel, through society and church. Faith allows God's people to be creative in their activities in the world, a world in which God is present and at work. To be faithful in one's calling is a freeing and fulfilling thing. It blesses not only the neighbor, but also the one who endeavors to be faithful. It assures the Christian that there is meaning and purpose in the ordinary tasks of his or her daily life.

The impact of Luther's teaching

Luther's forceful teaching on vocation had an enormous impact in helping individuals in his generation experience a new sense of dignity in their labors, learning to view them as activities that were at the same time God-pleasing and useful in God's world. Louis Almen, in the article, "Vocation in a Post-Vocational Age," wrote: "Luther's teaching on 'the calling' was liberating, giving new stature to the laity and providing new motivation, guidance and significance to daily occupations."[22]

Luther's views on vocation and the nature of work were incorporated into the confessional documents of the Lutheran Church. Philipp Melanchthon wrote in article 27 of the *Apology of the Augsburg Confession:*

If we follow this, the monastic life will be no more a state of perfection than the life of a farmer or an artisan. These, too, are states for acquiring perfection. All people, whatever their calling, should seek perfection, that is, growth in the fear of God, in faith, in the love for their neighbor, and in similar spiritual virtues.[23]

Luther's teaching also influenced the theologies of John Calvin and those who followed him. In the writings of subsequent Calvinist and Puritan theologians, however, a subtle transformation began to occur. Luther taught that all Christians are called to serve God *in* their occupations and that they respond to this call by loving their neighbors. These later writers, on the other hand, declared that God calls people *to* their occupations and that they respond to this call by performing their work with diligence and devotion. Thus, duty and hard work were elevated as God-pleasing virtues in and of themselves. Industrious workers were told to expect success and prosperity as marks of God's favor. Martin Luther, by contrast, had warned his readers that faithful Christian living brings with it the cross.

This reinterpretation of Luther's teaching paved the way for the so-called Protestant work ethic that was to play such a strong role in American life. In the process, the word vocation gradually came to be understood merely as a synonym for career or occupation. Once again, people envisioned a hierarchy of callings—since some occupations were more prestigious and yielded more prosperity than others.

Eventually, those who rejected the concept of a God who is involved in the lives of people continued to espouse the ideals of diligence and hard work and to promise the rewards of success and prosperity as ends in themselves. They professed their faith in economic laws rather than in God. In this way, ironically, vocation came to do exactly the opposite of what Luther had intended: namely, to aid the fracturing of Sunday and Monday for many people.

In today's postindustrial world, Martin Luther's understanding of vocation has disappeared in large part from the minds of people, Christian and non-Christian alike. People engage in "jobs," sometimes seeking from them ultimate meaning and at other times enduring them as utterly meaningless. In the next chapter, I will explore the possibility of reclaiming Luther's vocation teaching as a tool for helping Christians today rediscover the powerful role their faith can play in bringing meaning to their work.

For reflection

1. What does your baptism mean to you? How can the daily affirmation, "I am a baptized child of God," make a difference in the way you approach the day's responsibilities?
2. What is created through your daily work? Is it something tangible like a widget or something intangible like good will? How does knowing that you are an agent in God's ongoing work of creation make you feel?
3. Make a list of all the roles (stations, walks in life) that describe your life. Who is served as you carry out the responsibilities of these roles? Reflect on Luther's affirmation that these roles represent concrete expressions of God's call to you.

4

The Value of Luther's Teaching for Today

In our experience, as a person develops the capacity for critical reflection on his or her life's work, very often he or she begins to be clear about God's calling.[1]

The previous chapter outlined Martin Luther's understanding of the calling or vocation of all Christians as a consequence of their baptism into Christ. As heirs of Luther's teaching—a teaching that encouraged believers of his time to appreciate the value of their normal daily work as an act of service to God, a teaching that subsequently was reinterpreted in ways that would have horrified the reformer—a question we must address is: Can this teaching still (or again) be a catalyst that helps church members appreciate the connection between their church life and their daily lives, between their faith and their work, between their Sunday morning activities and the activities that occupy their time the rest of the week? Although there are those who would say otherwise, I believe the answer is "yes."

On the one hand, we have a resource in the writings of Martin Luther that can affirm us in our labors, reminding us that they are God-pleasing because they are neighbor-serving. On the other hand, we are also subject to all the forces that subtly redefined and drained the power from Luther's original understanding of vocation. In *Theological and Biblical Perspectives on the Laity*, Herman Stuempfle complains:

Our problem today is not so much the sacralization of vocation for a few, but its secularization for all. Vocation usually means, quite simply, one's job. We speak of vocational counseling, vocational schools, or vocational rehabilitation without conscious reference to the vertical dimension which informed Luther's understanding of the Christian's calling. For him, the little sphere of daily work and duty was located within the immense horizon of God's overarching command and promise. Our question today is whether we can help persons in the complex, technological, often depersonalized milieu of work to see their jobs or professions as their calling under God.[2]

Critiques of Luther's teaching

There are a number of contemporary observers of the church who dismiss the present day value of Luther's insight regarding the vocation of all the baptized. As Stuempfle notes, we live in a world far different from the one in which Martin Luther railed against the privileged position of those in ecclesiastical offices, who alone were perceived to have a God-given calling. Monastic withdrawal from the world poses little threat to the church today. In addition, people in 21st-century secular culture care little about doctrine. Luther's teachings in particular—framed, as they often are, in paradox—are difficult to grasp and often perceived as too esoteric for the average modern Christian.

Critics note that most people in the Western world have far more work options than Martin Luther possibly could have imagined. When my daughters began college, the dean of students, in his remarks to the parents, suggested that, on average, the young men and women will likely change their careers (not just their jobs) as often as five times. How does this reality fit with Luther's assertion that God has called a person in his or her present walk of life and he or she should stay in that walk of life?

Some contemporary church leaders worry that the teaching on vocation can be misused to oppose the mobility of workers. To do so discourages those whose daily work feels like a wearying rut that does little to tap their abilities, edify their neighbors, or glorify God.

Certainly, there have been more and less desirable occupations in every age. The scullery maids of the 16th century, for example, probably found little reason for pride or pleasure in their labors. One wonders, however, if Martin Luther could have anticipated the repetitive life of an assembly-line worker or the sense of meaninglessness experienced by laborers who have never seen the final product of their work and so have little sense of how their daily efforts contribute to any good greater than the meager enhancement of their own checkbooks when payday comes.

Central to Luther's teaching on vocation was his emphasis on God's call to the Christian to deny one's self and "bear the cross" in his or her daily work. Luther saw this as an honor for believers as well as a necessary implication of a daily return to baptism through which the old person dies with Christ as the redeemed person rises to new life. Since the 16th century, however, the summons to take up the cross and bear it bravely has been used in insidious ways—to keep people in oppressive situations. In this way, the appeal to the cross demeans, rather than affirms those who find themselves trapped in abusive systems.

The above critiques of Luther's vocation teaching are really of two types. The first suggests that Luther's teaching doesn't fit any more. Today's world of work is just too different from the world in which the reformer lived. A new paradigm is needed to encourage Christians to relate their faith to their daily labors. The second type of critique points out the fact that Luther's teaching has been misused—to justify the *status quo*, to encourage quietism toward societal injustice, and to counsel a passive acceptance of one's less than desirable station in life.

Regarding the first type of critique, it is, of course, important that we do not forget that Martin Luther was a product of his time and that he was responding to a specific concern within the limits and possibilities of the culture in which he lived. Luther's writings are not part of an immutable canon, after all. At the same time, we need not dismiss the wisdom of his insights or the transforming impact they had on those who heard them for the first time. We can appreciate the essence of what Luther affirmed even as we take into consideration the differences between his context and our own.

It was noted in the last chapter that when Luther urged the faithful to remain in their calling, his concern was not that there be no change or improvement in the lot of the Christian worker, but rather that the structures of society be honored and maintained over against the monastic tendency to denigrate those structures as inherently evil and to withdraw from them into a supposedly holier way of life. Luther insisted that the true vocation of the Christian, to honor God through service to the neighbor, could take various forms, each one of which would continuously help the Christian grow in faith by driving him or her to God in prayer. Such a notion is still a powerfully freeing insight to people today, even if the content and context of their work changes over time.

The second type of critique noted above is more of a commentary on the human propensity to pervert all great insights than it is a dismissal of the teaching on vocation as Luther redefined it. Martin Luther, of all theologians, recognized clearly the tendency for human beings to experience life from a self-serving, rather than God-serving or neighbor-serving perspective. It may be true that subsequent theological developments robbed Luther's doctrine of much of its power, but these distortions are not inherent in the doctrine itself. Rather, they are reminders of the enduring need for the Reformation's motto: *Ecclesia reformata et semper reformanda*—"the church reformed and always reforming." The church must be persistent in reexamining its teachings, keeping them centered in the proclamation of God's grace, respectful of God's law, and attentive to God's call to faith and faithful living.

It is precisely the subsequent misuses of Luther's teaching that encourage believers today to return repentant to a reconsideration of the important presuppositions that lay beneath it in the first place:

- God's creation is not a once and done activity, but a good and on-going reality in which every Christian is privileged to participate
- God is concerned with and wants to be involved in the whole of people's lives, not just their acts of piety
- daily living is a constant struggle between good and evil, driving the Christian back to the meaning of his or her baptism
- one's neighbor—broadly interpreted—is the beneficiary of the Christian's labors, providing a corrective to the self-centeredness that distorts so much of life in human society

In reaffirming these presuppositions today, we can discard the ways in which Luther's teaching has been misused and once again discover a renewed sense of meaning and purpose in our lives at work.

Elton Trueblood, a 20th century pioneer in reclaiming Luther's insight about God's concern for all of life, calls our attention to

> . . .the sense of joy that comes to a believer who is convinced that, humble as he is, he is a partner of the Living God, helping minutely in the work of creation. There is a world of difference between a building operation in which the workmen, however competent they may be, have their eyes on the clock, and one in which the workmen see their total task as a holy calling. . . .

The word "vocation" has been debased in the modern world by being made synonymous with "occupation," but it is one of the gains of our time that the old word is beginning to regain its original meaning of "calling."[3]

The enduring value of Luther's teaching

The above critiques and responses aside, perhaps the most compelling argument for the enduring value of Luther's teaching on vocation is the impact it continues to make in the lives of Christian men and women today, people who—like their 16th-century counterparts—experience the teaching as a new insight over against a modern "Babylonian captivity," the captivity of daily life and work to the idols of success and self-advancement. Carter Lindberg states: "American culture and life is no less mired in a 'piety of achievement' than the medieval culture and life that Luther addressed."[4] In contradistinction to this piety of achievement, Martin Luther offered a framework that can still help Christians find meaning and purpose in their work—to appreciate its value and to keep it from becoming all-consuming. In this way, the teaching on vocation provides a corrective for many of the 21st-century's unhealthy understandings of daily work.

There is a certain idolatry in the way many people view their work. They assume that their significance as people is linked inexorably to their choice of a career and the success they enjoy in it. They become "company people" whose first and, perhaps, only loyalty is to the firm. They do not have a perspective that helps them guard against compulsive and unhealthy overwork. Gain and glory, remuneration and recognition become the twin measures of genuine success. Satisfaction is found in "how things are going"—a far more precarious commodity than the certainty of one's relationship with God.

Seeing one's labors as an expression of a God-given vocation puts the modern tendency to turn work and its fruits into idols into a larger perspective. It helps place boundaries on ambition. It reminds us that work is inherently neither a curse nor an end in itself, but merely one of several arenas in the life of a believer in which God can be honored and one's neighbors served. Daily work is an activity. It is not that which gives ultimate value to a person's life. Nor is it the source of his or her identity.

God calls believers to use their gifts and their energies, but these gifts and energies do not establish the worth of persons. Individuals have value because God values them. The meaning of their lives is not imprisoned in their work. Such a reminder is a tremendous source of encouragement for getting through times of job loss and transition, for adjusting to retirement, and for coping when there is little sense of glamour or fulfillment to be found in one's labors.

In the article, "Work and Meaning," Marc Kolden, an advocate of resurrecting and affirming Luther's vocation teaching for contemporary Christians, writes:

> Faith in God means that we can take delight in our work and savor the meaning we find in it. Work can be a source of great joy, and achievement at work usually contributes to self-esteem. Through work we can find a niche in society whereby we contribute, use, and develop our abilities. At the same time, we are much more than our work, and we should not expect our work to lend more meaning to life than any created reality can. In fact, because we live in a world permeated not only by created goodness but also by sin, we may find ourselves hating or resisting aspects of our work God wants to put to use. Reflective faith can even find meaning in this. Martin Luther spoke of a "cross" as present in every calling, an aspect of the calling itself. . . . This notion of a cross in one's calling can assist us in making sense of failure, frustration, conflict, and even tragedy in our work.

> We do not usually think of such negative experiences as giving any-
> thing "meaning," but Luther would advise us that this is a realistic way
> to look at life and work; therefore, these experiences, too, belong to
> the meaning of our work.[5]

Kolden can write these words because he knows that, according to Luther, the meaning of work is found not in its ease or
pleasantness, or even in its tangible results. Meaning is found in
the extent to which our working drives us back to the ultimate
source of meaning—our relationship with Christ, through whom
we learn and are empowered to serve our neighbors and our community through our labors.

Vocation provides a corrective for the rampant individualism
and self-focus of modern life as it encourages believers to relate
their activities to the common good, not just their own good. The
real questions for Christians to ask regarding their daily work are
not, "How much do I make?" or "Will I be promoted?" or "Will
my efforts be appreciated?", but rather "What contribution am I
making?" and "About what will I feel proud to tell my grandchil-
dren someday?"

Martin Luther's focus on serving one's neighbor and the common good helps Christian evaluate the ethical decisions they are
called to make in the workplace. It becomes a test for making
sense of those gray areas in which it is unclear what is right and
what is wrong. The fact that Luther relates his teaching on vocation to baptism and justification—our work as a response to God's
gracious work in us—also allows Christian workers to acknowledge that sometimes they make bad decisions for which they must
seek God's forgiveness. Martin Luther's famous advice to Philipp
Melanchthon: "Be a sinner and sin boldly, but believe and rejoice
in Christ even more boldly" applies to the arena of daily work no
less than to that of church reform.[6]

Confidence that God has called them in their daily labors and is concerned with their daily labors offers Christian workers a criterion for dealing with the tough decision of whether to stay in their present position or seek another: "Is my work inherently dishonorable? Does it cheat my neighbors, rather than improve their lives? Does it waste my time and talent? Is it possible to bring glory to God through this job, or is it just marking time?" By placing the meaning of daily work on a higher plane, the teaching of vocation not only helps believers find a sense of dignity in their activities, it also gives them a sense of when to move on, trusting that God is with them.

A task for today's church

I am convinced that an essential task for the church is to develop more resources targeted for the average adult believer that affirm Martin Luther's teaching on vocation. The more church members are equipped to listen for the good news that God is active in the mundane world of work and that God calls people to become aware of how their own work serves God, the more the gap between Sunday and Monday can be erased.

Vocation reminds believers that they can serve God in the fields of business, education, science, healthcare, and politics just as surely as they serve God through their worship. There is no divide between sacred and secular activities, because all of life is the locus of God's activity. Those who discover this experience a greater sense of balance between the expression of their faith through worship, prayer, and service in their church and the expression of their faith through faithful daily life and work. Strong support and encouragement from a caring Christian community is needed if this is to become more of a conscious and effective part of believers' self-understanding.

The ELCA has taken steps to acknowledge the importance of being more intentional about teaching people that God's call embraces the whole of their lives, that their faith is an asset that brings meaning to their work, and that their work is an aspect of their vocation to serve God and neighbor. The 1993 ELCA statement, *Together for Ministry*, does not give central place to the topic of vocation. It does, however, declare:

> God calls all Christians to a life of vocation. To have a "vocation" means to live out one's call. For Christians, that call is answered in the structures of daily life—family, work, state, service to the neighbor, care of creation—as the setting in which to live out their identity in the gospel.[7]

The ELCA's "Model Constitution for Congregations" challenges the Christian community to:

> Nurture its members in the Word of God so as to grow in faith and hope and love, to see daily life as the primary setting for the exercise of their Christian calling, and to use the gifts of the Spirit for their life together and for their calling in the world.[8]

More effort needs to be given on the congregational level to translate these official statements into reality. It is not easy to erase the gap between Sunday and Monday in the minds of many church members, particularly when that divide has been and continues to be reinforced by the institutional church itself. The notion that God is concerned about and has a calling for men and women of faith within the whole range of their life's activities requires consistent and persistent reinforcement.

Resources that promote the teaching on vocation will begin where people are—not with the articulation of theological concepts, but with the questions and struggles and hopes and dreams raised in their day-to-day labors. Such resources will be most effective as they mirror the concrete, down-to-earth approach of Martin Luther himself, an approach that captured and set on fire imaginations of ordinary Christians who previously had given little thought to the relationship of their Sunday faith and their Monday work.

Still today, many of the baptized struggle to understand how their spirituality can play more of a role in the whole of their lives. They may spend hours in church, worshipping and serving, and still leave feeling empty because they don't know how their Christian activities intersect with all the other activities that place such a large claim on their time and energies.

God has given the church good news that makes it possible for all people to live above the despair that can so easily characterize modern living. This good news does not find its power in an invitation for people to retreat from the hectic character of their of daily schedules and routines. Rather, it gives them a new perspective that brings them dignity and purpose within those schedules and routines. It is the calling of the institutional church to explore and use every means possible to proclaim this good news and translate it into a reality that God's people can grasp and apply to their everyday life and work. The next chapter will outline some practical steps that a congregation can take to incorporate an affirmation of Luther's teaching on vocation into the whole of its life.

For reflection

1. To what extent are you affected by society's tendency to base self-worth on achievement? How can the teaching on vocation provide a counterbalance to this?

2. How does the teaching on vocation give deeper meaning to both the time you spend "at church" and the time you spend "being the church" wherever you are?
3. What kinds of ethical decisions or dilemmas have you faced in your work? How can your faith serve as a resource for making difficult decisions?

5

Strategies for Supporting the Vocation of Christians at Work

A woman, asked about her family, said, "I have two grown children. One is in business; the other is serving the Lord." Those who work at "secular" jobs, whether in business or other professions, are not always seen as active Christian servants. Some are even regarded as second class citizens in the kingdom of God. Not all of us are gifted to be pastors or missionaries. Nonetheless, we too have been given occupational assignments through which we can be God's junior partners in meeting the daily needs that help sustain God's creation. Scripture suggests that our daily work is a calling through which we can exercise the gifts God has given us.[1]

The first two chapters dealt with the reality that many active church members often fail to perceive the connection between their normal, daily routines and the faith they profess as Christians. Along with the woman above, they simply never have thought about careers in business (or many other careers) as being opportunities to serve the one they call Lord. Ironically, the institutional church is often one of the culprits in discouraging its members from making the connection between Sunday and Monday. Chapters 3 and 4 proposed a reaffirmation of the Lutheran teaching on vocation as a resource for assisting believers to find in their baptisms not only God's offer of grace and salvation, but also God's call to recognize every aspect of their lives, including their daily work, as an arena in which they can respond to God in thanksgiving and serve as partners with God in the ongoing work of creation.

Reflecting on the meaning and value of her daily work, Barbara Jeffries writes:

> We all have a vocation—a calling to a unique purpose—not just those who are called to the religious life. What could be more adventurous than living out our call in the paid work we do? What could be more exciting, more fun, or more humbling? What would our workplaces look like if everyone were living their call?[2]

The purpose of this chapter is to explore how congregations can present Luther's teaching on vocation in a new way—not as a stale religious doctrine with little present-day value, but as a framework for helping church members experience their daily work as part of the adventure of faithful Christian living.

In its worship life, its educational ministry, its fellowship times, and in its very structure, a congregation ought to guide believers toward an affirmation of the following truths:

1. God calls me to express my baptismal identity through everything I do—including the time I spend at work.
2. I am never alone as I go about my work. God is with me and God's people are available to support me.
3. My normal, everyday actions serve God and others. They contribute to the good of God's world. Through them, God is at work.
4. Despite my best efforts, I sometimes fail. I make foolish and counterproductive decisions. Because of God's grace, there is forgiveness and the promise of a new beginning.

Those truths sound clear and simple enough. The key is to reinforce them in realistic ways, recognizing the complex issues and questions that arise when Christians endeavor to be intentional about relating their faith and their work. Here is a partial list of concerns that I have heard believers struggle with as they think about their work in the context of God's call to faithful living:

- *Competitiveness* at work and society's preoccupation with winning. Can a Christian be ambitious? Is it okay to be proud of one's accomplishments?
- *Job transitions and insecurity.* What should a Christian consider when making the decision to change jobs? What does the notion of God's call to be an active participant in the ongoing work of creation mean in times of job loss?
- *Relationships at work.* How does God call Christians to relate to co-workers, colleagues, superiors, staff, clients, customers? How can they maintain the dignity of each individual in systems that are predisposed to treating people like numbers on a balance sheet—as assets or liabilities whose sole value lies in their ability to increase profitability?
- *Salary and benefits.* How should a Christian handle the issue of salary negotiation? Is it okay to demand more? How does one's faith relate to his or her lifestyle choices?
- *Maintaining boundaries.* How can Christians cope with the never-ending demands of their jobs? By what criteria do they set priorities and draw limits?
- *Working at home.* How can the church affirm the worth of those who use their energies primarily for homemaking and child-raising? How can individuals who spend most of their waking hours in isolation address their relationship needs?
- *Meaningless employment.* What should be the believer's response when work seems like a burden, not a gift? What is the church's role in supporting those at the bottom of the economic ladder who are trapped in unrewarding and, sometimes, dehumanizing jobs?

- *Ethics in the workplace.* How can a Christian's value system help him or her make difficult decisions, especially when the system is pushing him or her toward an unethical decision?

To provide a forum for addressing concerns such as these, I created a weekend retreat experience for adults that uses scripture, the writings of Martin Luther, and case studies of real on-the-job issues to help participants reflect on their daily work from the point of view of God's call. The approach of the retreat is inductive, featuring significant opportunities for participants to speak about their work experiences—their joys and satisfactions, their questions and frustrations. The church's teaching on vocation is offered as a tool to help them wrestle with their questions and frustrations and place their joys and satisfactions into a larger interpretive framework. The role of the retreat leaders is not to give easy, pious-sounding answers to complicated real-life dilemmas. Rather it is to listen, to affirm the complex nature of the workday tensions people experience, to draw out the wisdom of the group to help fellow believers deal with those tensions, and to encourage all participants to examine the concerns they raise from the point of view of their faith. (The author has developed a retreat design, including eight worship experiences and six group sessions. See "Resources," p. 95.)

I cannot stress enough the power of sympathetic listening as way of supporting Christian workers. After a meeting of an adult study course focusing on issues of faith and daily work, one group member told me that the most powerful moments for him are those times when we leave the stated agenda and simply listen to each other. There is no other venue in his life where such supportive listening takes place. It is too dangerous for him to be open about his feelings at work. The co-worker with whom he speaks today might one day be his boss. To offer mutual supportive listening is an important component of God's call.

Reflecting on the implications of vocation and exploring the relationship between faith and daily work represents a life-long journey for believers, a journey encumbered by numerous obstacles. Certainly one retreat experience—particularly one that revolves around an insight that most find brand new—will accomplish little if it is not accompanied by a variety of opportunities to reinforce the affirmation that God is involved in the everyday and has called the baptized to lives of service not only within the church, but also in the world. In other words, congregations should strive to integrate the teaching on vocation into every part of their life and ministry.

Over the past fifteen years, I have led a number of workshops for congregations reflecting this perspective. In the process I have discovered two things: First, pastoral leaders must be convinced that the primary focus of the congregation's mission lies outside its walls and activities. They must be energetic in helping believers discover what God's call means for them in the context of their daily lives and work. If the pastor is preoccupied with providing for the programmatic needs of the congregation above all else, most members will come to assume that the congregation is the sole arena in which they are called to serve God.

Second, many different and complementary strategies for affirming the vocation of the baptized must be employed. Indeed, they must be employed consistently and persistently if folks are going to get the message that the main purpose of the church is not to draw in the energy of its members, but rather to send them out—renewed by God's grace, empowered by the Holy Spirit, and equipped through the congregation's ministries—to celebrate God's daily presence in every place in which they find themselves.

What follows are a number of strategies that encourage Christians to listen for God's call to them. Most I have used in the congregations I have served as pastor. Most of them are not difficult. Few congregations would have difficulty adapting them for their own use. Typically, these strategies involve a subtle shift in the congregation's (or the pastor's) priorities rather than a total upheaval of congregational life.

Few of these strategies are original with me. Nor is this list exhaustive. Descriptions of many of them, and many others as well, appear in published materials. I recommend, in particular:

- *Ministry in Daily Life,* a book by William Diehl outlining the ways in which the congregation to which he belongs has endeavored to educate and motivate its members to explore the connections between their Sunday morning activities and their weekday lives (The Alban Institute, 1996).
- *Working: Making a Difference in God's World,* a notebook of resources, updated periodically, that delineates a wide variety of tactics that have been used effectively in congregations (ELCA, 1995).
- The ministry in daily life internet site of the Episcopal Church in the U.S.A. (www.episcopalchurch.org/ministry/daily). This extensive web site offers tools for assessing the extent to which a congregation is inward or outward focused. It also offers a myriad of suggestions for raising the consciousness of members with regard to how their baptismal call relates to their daily life and work activities.

Worship ministry

Some congregations have special worship emphases on a particular Sunday each year to honor the daily work of their members. On these Sundays, congregational members may be invited to wear their work clothes to worship. They may also bring objects they use in the course of their work and place them around the altar as symbols of the ways in which they serve God, God's people, and God's world each day. Hymns, scripture readings, prayers, and the sermon (often given by someone other than the pastor) focus on the subject of vocation. One appropriate occasion for such an emphasis is the Sunday of Labor Day weekend.

Special emphases can be meaningful, but only if they are reinforced regularly. It is far more effective to include the concept of vocation in every worship experience. This can be done by:

- *Paying attention to the content of sermons.* Preachers can learn from Jesus, who in his teaching and his parables, had much to say about everyday activities and relationships. To discover what work-related issues are on people's minds, preachers should spend time talking with parishioners—asking them what is going on in their work and listening to the concerns they raise. Also, preachers should endeavor to speak positively about the world of work.

- *Paying attention to the content of prayers.* Most congregations include prayers for those who are sick, grieving, or in special need. They may pray regularly for their own ministries and those of the larger church. It is also important to celebrate the joys and commend to God the challenges that people are experiencing in the performance of their work. One way of doing this is to focus each week on a specific occupational group and to ask those in that field of work for their prayer requests. In his book, *Ministry in Daily Life*, William Diehl suggests eight occupational groupings: education, health care, business and industry, homemaking, science and technology, retirement, public service, the arts. To these I have added agriculture. Each congregation can develop its own list of occupational groupings that is appropriate to its composition and that of its surrounding community.

- *Paying attention to who is recognized or commissioned.* Just as those who are elected to special offices or who volunteer for significant ministries within the congregation are recognized through a rite of installation, a brief rite can be observed periodically to commission church members to exercise their calling in the course of their daily activities. Such a rite can be based on the liturgy for the affirmation of baptism. Each time a commissioning service is held, it can focus on a specific occupational group.

- *Paying attention to the church year calendar.* Many of the minor festivals and commemorations in the church year calendar celebrate individuals who used their gifts in specific occupations to the glory of God—musicians, artists, etc. This can be the springboard for reminding worshippers that God's gifts bring with them a call to use those gifts for the benefit of others and to honor God.

- *Employing alternative proclamation techniques.* A number of fine dramas designed for use in worship focus on God's call to live faithfully day-by-day. Worship leaders can also interview individuals regarding their joys and challenges in the workplace, allowing other worshippers to empathize with the way each individual experiences God's presence and endeavors to live as a Christian at work. One congregation with which I have worked has a weekly theme song, "Go Out To Serve," that worshippers sing at the conclusion of each worship experience to reinforce the connection between the liturgy and their daily lives.

- *Reminding worshippers that worship ministry is not limited to those activities that happen in the sanctuary.* Pastors can encourage congregational members to pray for one another daily, focusing on concerns from the workplace. Members can be assured that even when they are scattered in their daily places, the prayers of fellow believers will continue to strengthen them.

Educational ministry

The Lutheran Church of the Holy Spirit in Emmaus, Pennsylvania, of which William Diehl is a member, has a "Center for Faith and Life" that orients the entire adult educational curriculum around a daily life focus. Several courses of study are offered each Sunday. Few congregations are large enough to have leaders or participants to make such a center possible. However, there are things that congregations of any size can do to support the Christian teaching on vocation through their educational ministry. These include:

- *Hold a "gifts identification" workshop.* Various tools exist for aiding Christians in identifying their specific gifts and discovering how they can and do employ these gifts. It is important to stress that the gifts God has given them are meant to serve God in every aspect of life, not just through the official ministries of the church.

- *Orient adult Christian education around daily life and work issues.* Even if this can not happen with the sophistication that Diehl describes, any educational program can take into account the reality that congregational members have concerns they would like to explore in the context of their faith, issues such as: ethics in the workplace, what is an appropriate lifestyle for Christians in a culture preoccupied with unbounded affluence, and other concerns mentioned at the beginning of this chapter. Start with the world and weave in the word.

- *Promote retreat experiences and workshops.* Provide opportunities for Christians from various congregations to gather for the purpose of exploring daily life and work issues in the context of their faith.

- *Hold periodic "occupation fairs" for children and youth.* Adults from the congregation speak about their work—what excites them, what challenges them, and how they make the connections between their work and their faith.

Fellowship and support ministry

Fellowship and support ministries offer church members a cadre of fellow believers with whom they can form relationships in a casual setting. In support groups, people can develop the level of trust needed to be open and honest in acknowledging the times when faith and life don't seem to connect. Group members can also encourage one another to recognize their potential and hold each other accountable for the use of their gifts. Possibilities for support group ministry include:

- *Groups organized around specific occupational types or life situations.* The congregation I serve as pastor has, from time to time, hosted a support group for stay-at-home mothers. The group gives them an opportunity for friendly conversation and a forum in which to discuss common concerns.

- *Groups organized around people's passions—the kinds of activities that excite and motivate them.* Group members are encouraged to celebrate their passions as energies given to them by God. Together they explore the ways in which their pursuit of these passions brings glory to God.

Social ministry strategies

One of the concerns raised in chapter 2 is that for a number of people, particularly those on the lowest end of the socioeconomic ladder, daily work is not a source of fulfillment. Rather, it often seems like a necessary evil at best. Folks can feel trapped in dead-end jobs that bear little relationship to their gifts and passions. For others, job security is at an all-time low. The threat of impending layoff keeps anxiety levels high and impedes any attempt to see one's occupation as an arena for exercising God's call. To be consistent in its affirmation that the Christian faith is connected to the mundane concerns of daily work, the congregation, through its ministries of social concern can:

- *Advocacy ministry.* Engage in advocacy ministry for those trapped in unskilled jobs, working to insure that they are compensated properly and not taken advantage of.
- *Community ministries.* Help provide for the needs of those whose income is barely at subsistence levels. This can be done by participating in community ministries that offer career counseling and teach interviewing skills.
- *Promote programs that provide child care at reasonable cost.* Include round-the-clock child care for those whose opportunity to enter the work force is in second or third shift jobs.
- *Assist people who are in times of job transition.* In a support group setting, people who are between jobs can encourage each other.
- *Job Networking.* Endeavor to establish a communications network that can assist participants in finding new jobs.

Pastoral ministry

Chapter 2 encouraged parish pastors to spend more time listening to congregational members—allowing them to brag and complain about the things that are going on in their lives. By asking questions and listening empathetically, the pastor can model the fact that the Christian faith is concerned about more than just what happens in the church building. This supportive act of listening also fills a great void, especially in the lives of people who work in competitive business settings in which baring one's soul may be seen as a sign of weakness or vulnerability and may become an impediment against advancement. As pastors give members an opportunity to be open and reflective and assist them in making the connection between Sunday and Monday, recognizing how God's call can be lived at home and at work as well as at church, it is helpful to:

- *Visit people at their places of work.* It has long been the practice of pastors to conduct home visitations. Many congregational members spend more time at work than they do at home. Interacting with members in the "home court" of their office or work station, reinforces the teaching that the church (that is, their community of fellow believers) is interested in what believers do in their daily occupations.

- *Exercise care when speaking to congregational members about their work, or lack of it.* It is important not to use cliches or speak disparagingly about tasks that individuals may find very meaningful or fulfilling. Relating to those who are experiencing the stress of job transition requires particular sensitivity and tact.

Communication ministry

Congregations use a variety of means to communicate with their members—oral announcements at worship, bulletin boards, newsletters, Web sites. It is important that each of these avenues of communication also reflects the dual focus of congregational life: reporting not only the things that are happening within the church building and its programs, but also the things that members are doing when they are scattered far from one another. Congregations can highlight the ways in which God's call relates to daily life and work by:

- *Newsletters.* Including regularly in their newsletters a profile describing the average day of a member who exemplifies what it means to live faithfully.

- *Bulletin boards.* Making sure that bulletin boards include spaces for posting articles highlighting the weekday achievements of members—promotions, significant milestones at work or school or in volunteer work in the community.

- *Correspondence.* Having congregational leaders or staff write congratulatory letters to members who celebrate milestones at work or school.
- *Mission statements.* Including the concept of vocation—as it relates to daily life and work—in the mission statement of the congregation and articulating this often in describing the congregation's priorities.

Organizational life

Congregations that are top-heavy with structure—maintaining a huge array of committees and taskforces—may find it difficult to focus intentionally on God's call for members to be faithful in daily life and work. There are just so many opportunities to use their energies within the congregation. To remind those heavily involved in congregational life that God's call to them extends beyond the church's official programs, congregations can:

- *Periodically examine their structure to determine what task groups are no longer necessary.* Schedule committee meetings only when there is work to be done. Take care not to over-work the limited pool of volunteers from which most congregations draw.
- *Train volunteer recruiters.* Encourage those who recruit volunteers to be sensitive to folks who decline the invitation to be more active at church because of home or work obligations—affirming them in their efforts to serve God through such obligations, rather than making them feel guilty because they cannot take on a responsibility in the congregation.
- *Honor the reality that those who participate in committees and organizations of the congregation also have many commitments*

in the other arenas of their lives. In my congregation, the closing prayer at every meeting takes into account the fact that people are leaving the church building, but are going to other important facets of their lives—home, work, rest, etc. The prayer, therefore, includes a petition asking for God's guidance and support as they attend to these other activities.

The above strategies are useful for any congregation, pastor, church leader, or individual believer who is serious about the task of connecting more intentionally the faith professed each week in worship and the tasks of everyday living. Behind all of the strategies lies a fundamental attitude that God is active in the world and that one's "worldly" work represents an opportunity to serve and honor God. Those who are intent on affirming the vocation of Christians in daily life and work will strive to create a congregational climate that supports the twin notions that God has called all the baptized to faithful living and that this call to faithful living is answered at church, at home, at work, and at rest.

For reflection

1. Reread the four statements on page 70. How can you incorporate each of these affirmations into your understanding of your daily work?
2. Where do you look for support for the issues and challenges you face at work? What helps you get through the bad days? In what ways can your congregation be more supportive of you in your daily work?
3. Reflect on the lists of strategies presented in this chapter. Which ones are already being done in your faith community? What one or two would you like to see initiated? What role can you play in helping to create a congregational climate that supports the connecting of faith and daily life?

6

Sunday and Monday in Sync

For a variety of sociological reasons, the mission and ministry of the Christian church in the twenty-first century will fall on the shoulders of the laity. The good news is that the Christian laity are already located in strategic positions to carry out this ministry—in offices, factories, homes, schools, government—in short, in the world. The bad news is that the Christian laity have been raised in a church in which they have been largely passive. It is a church that has urged the laity to become active exclusively in congregational life and has left them to fend for themselves in their weekday world.[1]

With these words, William Diehl begins, "We Are Called," the final chapter of his book, *Ministry in Daily Life*. In one paragraph, Diehl accents both the opportunities and the challenges involved in nurturing a body of Christian believers who are aware of God's call to them and who are intent on seeking ways to express that call as they go about the routines and the tasks of their daily lives.

God cares about the world, so much so that God continues to be at work in it. God is at work in and through the lives of people, all people—whether they are aware of it or not, whether they are Christian or not. How exciting it can be for believers to discover this activity of God where they least expect it, in the everyday. How affirming it is for them to realize that they are, in effect, agents of God in the ongoing work of creation and even "means of grace" as they function as the channels through which others experience God's love. How seldom do most congregations proclaim this provocative truth as they find their energies and priorities drawn inward to the various activities that, by necessity or by custom, take place to maintain the institution of the church. How difficult it is for many of the baptized to hear this truth, accustomed as often they are to experiencing their daily work merely as a necessity related primarily to "making a living."

In the previous chapter, I suggested that congregations and their leaders must be intentional and consistent in reinforcing the church's teaching on vocation and its application to the daily lives of its members. At least some part of the gathering times of the Christian community should be devoted to acknowledging and celebrating the sacred character of those times when the members of the body of Christ scatter to go about the routine tasks of daily living. This is a challenge, given the deeply rooted tendency of people to confine God and faith to places and actions traditionally perceived as religious.

As the church endeavors to address this challenge, it is important to celebrate the fact that there are members of congregations who do "get it." There are Christians who, hearing the teaching on vocation articulated and affirmed again and again, begin to develop the skills to listen for God's call to them in every aspect of their lives. They know that there is more to life than work—and they know that through their work they have a prime opportunity to express who they are as people created and gifted by God. They know that through their daily labors they provide a service to other people, whether directly or indirectly—and they know that in serving, they also honor God who has called them to do this very thing. They know that everything they do is affected by the fact that they are sinners—and they know that, in Christ, God offers them forgiveness and the possibility of bringing value even from their imperfect actions. All of this gives them a sense of resilience as they approach the routines of daily life and work as well as an attitude of expectation as opposed to the futility that characterizes the outlook of so many people in the workforce today.

In my work as a parish pastor, I have had the privilege of becoming acquainted with and learning from a number of congregational members who demonstrate the kind of life in which Sunday and Monday are in sync. I offer the first-person testimonies of three of them, both as paradigms of how Christians can approach daily work from the perspective of the church's teaching on vocation and as evidence of the qualitative difference such a perspective can make in a person's life. The first two testimonies are portions of audiotaped interviews I conducted for a doctor of ministry project. The third is part of a speech given at the 2001 assembly of the Northeastern Pennsylvania Synod (ELCA), of which I served as chaplain. The assembly sub-theme was, "Connect the faith you have with the life you lead." These three individuals come from different walks of life. All three are active in the congregation in different ways, based on their passions and gifts. All have a sense of how their church activities prepare them to find meaning in their work and how their work gives meaning to their involvement in the congregation.

Testimony 1:

Donald is an attorney in his late forties. His specialty is defending clients who have been injured on the job. Notice especially how his sense of call affects his perspective about the people for whom he works. Notice also his ability to articulate the importance of maintaining a rhythm between worship and work.

My question: In what sense do you experience a connection between your work and your calling as a Christian?

His answer: I see my calling as helping people who are down. So my ministry is to address the needs of people who are in need, usually who have financial hardship because of their injuries.

How many attorneys are doing that work? But my feeling is that I'm doing it for God. I'm doing it in an honest way, an honest approach, by working hard, by doing the most that I can, and doing it on a personal level. These aren't just people passing through my office from whom I hope to make money, but really people who I realize have a life, and for a short time I'm a part of that life and they're looking at me for strength. They're looking at me for honest answers and an honest approach. And that, as I see it, is my calling.

My question: Is there anything else you want to add about the relationship of your faith and daily work?

His answer: I have been getting to realize more and more that it is an endless seam. You don't have to wear it on your collar, but what I do at work is carrying out my faith and in my faith on Sunday morning I'm praying for my clients as well. So I see it all as doing God's work.

Testimony 2:

Dawn is the secretary to the postmaster of a large, regional post office. Her position is a hectic one. Although I visited her at work (over her lunch hour), I had to interview her at home because her office telephone rings almost constantly. Notice especially how Dawn speaks of looking to her faith for wisdom and discovering in her Christian identity a sense of inner peace. Notice also her appreciation for worship as a means for sorting through what she is experiencing in daily life.

My Question: Does being a Christian make a difference in your work and in your relationships with the people you meet at work?

Her response: Yes, it does, because in the morning I pray and I ask God to get me through the day, because I know I need that. The main thing I ask for all the time is wisdom to get through the day, even the little daily things, just to make the right decisions or just to guide me on how far I can take this.

I think that if I didn't truly believe that, there'd be no way I could handle it. There's some kind of inner peace I get from that or there's some kind of intervention that gives me input there.

My question: In what ways could your congregation be more supportive of you in your work life?

Her response: Well, I think what's really good is your sermons really touch base. I don't go in there and just listen to Bible stories and scriptures. You relate them to life and to modern day life, everyday life. So often I will say, that was so keyed in to exactly what I'm going through right now. Just the whole Sunday service, because that does carry you through the week. It's so important how a pastor does sermons. That helps tremendously.

Testimony 3:

Bob is trained in the sciences. For the last decade, he has worked in quality assurance for several manufacturing companies. Notice Bob's conscious efforts to seek God's will for him at work and in relationships. He prays about situations at work. He calls on the resources of his faith to help him put difficult experiences into perspective.

Over my years in the workplace, I have found that for many people including me, work plays an important role in defining who we are and how we feel about ourselves. Work shapes us to a greater or lesser extent depending on our personalities and life situation.

If workplace values are similar to ours, it is not difficult to take one's Sunday faith and transfer it to Monday and the rest of the week. But when the workplace encourages us and rewards us for doing things that would be in conflict with what "Jesus would do" if he were in the neighboring cubical, we can find ourselves making some poor choices. One of the challenges of my job life is finding ways to maintain my Christian values and find appropriate ways of acting during situations where the usual and customary reaction may be something less than Christ-like.

How to do that is the important question. I remind myself of God's love and grace and his forgiveness when I don't get it right. I remind myself that God not only created me but also everyone around me. Having these beliefs helps me respect others and reminds me that there are certain principles that should not be compromised. In my family we call these "hills to die on," and they are things such as being truthful, not hurting others, keeping your word and being respectful. Having these sets of beliefs and principles gives me some standards by which to judge my reactions to adversity.[2]

Some might quibble with the ways in which Donald, Dawn, and Bob speak about their vocation. They are not trained, after all, in the nuances of theological expression. I, on the other hand, celebrate their testimonies. The church in the 21st century can learn from Christians like them. These are people whose eyes are open to the good news that God is at work in the world and that God chooses to work, in part, through them and their ordinary activities. They take God to work with them, because, in truth, God is already there. They recognize those with whom they interact at work as neighbors whom God has called them to love. They evidence the importance of maintaining a rhythm between Sunday and Monday, between worship and work, each of which informs and deepens their involvement in the other. They know where to turn for help, guidance, perspective, forgiveness, and renewal in the face of daily routines where so much is beyond their control. They make the connection!

Donald, Dawn, and Bob don't just go to church. They are the church. They are the church seven days a week, wherever they happen to be.

The building in which the community of believers gathers is an important place. It is a place for corporate worship, a place where people can have their perspectives renewed through word and sacrament. It is a place for learning. It is a place for offering and receiving support. It is one place where Christians can find God. But it is not the only place in which God is calling.

The whole world is filled with God's activity. God's creative work continues—and God's people participate in that work through their constructive actions day-in and day-out, as they help to provide for the needs of their neighbors. The redemptive work of God continues—and God's people participate in that work as others perceive in them the witness of lives in which Sunday and Monday are unified.

Through the daily work of Christian individuals who have learned to appreciate the connection between the faith they hold and the lives they lead, who have been nurtured by their congregations and then sent out to perform their many and various everyday tasks, God is honored. Through their ability to listen to God's call to them as it embraces the totality of their lives, these same individuals experience a sense of dignity and vitality as they face the challenges of daily living. And through these individuals, the church makes an impact on the world.

For reflection

1. How does the teaching on vocation give deeper meaning to both the time you spend "at church" and the time you spend "being the church" wherever you are?

2. Most congregations have members like Donald, Dawn, and Bob. Who can be for you a role model of someone who integrates faith and daily living in healthy ways?

3. How has this book equipped you to listen more intentionally to God's call and experience it as an invitation to let your faith play a role in every aspect of your life?

Notes

Preface

1   David Dycus, "All in a Day's Work," *Readers Digest*, April 1991, p. 127.

Chapter 1: The Sunday–Monday Split

1   Gordon Preece. "Work," in *The Complete Book of Everyday Christianity*, ed. Robert J. Banks and R. Paul Stevens (Downers Grove: InterVarsity Press, 1997), p. 1127.

2   Richard Avery and Donald Marsh, "We Are the Church" (© 1972 Hope Publishing Co, Carol Stream, IL 60188). Use by permission.

3   Nelvin Vos, "The Vocation of the Laity," in *The New Church Debate*, ed. Carl Braaten (Minneapolis: Fortress Press, 1983), p. 98.

4   Patricia Page, *All God's People Are Ministers: Equipping Church Members for Ministry* (Minneapolis: Augsburg Fortress, 1993), p. 9.

5   The Evanston Report. (New York: Harper & Brothers, 1955), p. 168.

Chapter 2: How the Split Came to Be

1   Sally Simmel, "Invite a Friend to Work," in *The Call*, (ELCA, Division for Ministry, August 2001) p. 1.

2   Robert N. Bellah, Richard Madsen, William H. Sullivan, Ann Swidler, and Steve Tipton, *Habits of the Heart: Individualism and Commitment in American Life* (New York: Harper and Row, 1985), p. 204.

3   Ibid., p. 224.

4   Ibid., p. 16.

5 Patricia Page, *All God's People Are Ministers: Equipping Church Members for Ministry* (Minneapolis: Augsburg Fortress, 1993), p. 60.

6 Celia A. Hahn, "Where in the World is the Church," in *The Calling of the Laity*, ed. Verna J. Dozier (Washington, D.C.: The Alban Institute, 1988), p. 89.

7 Edward A. White, "The Sunday-Monday Gap: Resistances in Church and World to Connecting Faith and Work," in *Faith Goes to Work: Reflections from the Marketplace*, ed. Robert J. Banks (Washington, D.C.: The Alban Institute, 1993), p. 5.

8   William Diehl, *The Monday Connection: A Spirituality of Competence, Affirmation, and Support in the Workplace* (New York: Harper Collins, 1991), p. 12.

9   Jacqueline McMakin and Rhoda Nary, "Empowering the Ministries of the Laity: How Congregations Can Go About It," in *The Calling of the Laity*, ed. Verna J. Dozier, (Washington, D.C.: The Alban Institute, 1988), p. 126.

10 Elton Trueblood, *Your Other Vocation.* (New York: Harper Brothers, 1952), pp. 28-29.

Chapter 3: A Resource from Our Heritage

1   Martin Luther, WA10.1.1:308-309 (*Luthers Werke, Wiemar Ausgabe,* Kritische Gesamtausgabe, Weimar: Boehlau, 1883ff).

2   Jurgen Moltmann, "Reformation and Revolution." In *Martin Luther and the Modern Mind.* ed. Manfred Hoffmann, Toronto Studies in Theology, v. 22 (Lewiston, New York: The Edwin Mellen Press, 1985), p. 186.

3   Decretum Magistri Gratiani, in Corpus Iuris Canonici, v. 1. (Akademischen Druck- u. Verlagsanstalt Graz, 1955), p. 678.

4   Martin Luther, WA 37:480, (*Luthers Werke, Wiemar Ausgabe.* Kritische Gesamtausgabe, Weimar: Boehlau, 1883ff).

5   Martin Luther, LW 3:128, (*Luther's Works.* Ed. Jaroslav Pelikan and Helmut T. Lehmann. St. Louis: Concordia Publishing Company and Philadelphia: Fortress Press, 1955).

6   Ibid., LW 31:344.

7   Ibid., LW 44:127.

8   Ibid., LW 21:237.

9   Ibid., LW 3:321.

10 Ibid., LW 46:246.

11 *The Book of Concord: The Confession of the Lutheran Church,* eds. Robert Kolb and Timothy J. Wengert, (Minneapolis, MN: Fortress Press, 2000). p. 406.

12 Martin Luther, BA 5:463, (*Luthers Werke fur das Christliche Haus,* 4th Edition. Ed. Buchawald, Kawerau, Kostlin, Rade, Schneider, et.al. (Leipzig: M. Heinsius, Nachfolger Eger & Sievers, 1924).

13 Op.Cit., LW 6:10.

14 Op.Cit., Kolb, 389.

15 Op.Cit., WA 27:400.

16 Op.Cit., LW 3:217.

17 Ibid., LW 46:226.

18 Ibid., LW 46:246.

19 Ibid., LW 3:128.

20 Ibid., LW 3:62.

21 Ibid., LW 21:20.

22 Louis T. Almen, "Vocation in a Post-Vocational Age," *Word and World* vol. 4, no. 2, Spring 1984, p. 131.

23 Op.Cit., Kolb, 283.

Chapter 4: The Value of Luther's Teaching for Today

1 David Foy Crabtree, *The Empowering Church: How One Congregation Supports Lay People's Ministries in the World* (Washington, D.C.: The Alban Institute, 1989), p. 18.

2 Herman Stuempfle. "Theological and Biblical Perspectives on the Laity," (Chicago: Division for Ministry, ELCA, 1989), p. 10.

3 Elton Trueblood, *Your Other Vocation* (New York: Harper Brothers, 1952), p. 63.

4 Carter Lindberg, "The Ministry and Vocation of the Baptized." *Lutheran Quarterly*, Winter 1992, p. 396.

5 Marc Kolden, "Work and Meaning: Some Theological Reflections," *Interpretation* 48:3, July 1994, p. 269.

6 Op. Cit., LW 48:282.

7 *Together for Ministry* (Chicago: Division for Ministry, ELCA, 1993), p.14.

8 "Model Constitution for Congregations," (Chicago: Division for Ministry, ELCA, 1989), C4.02.e.

Chapter 5: Strategies for Supporting the Vocation of Christians at Work

1 Ben Sprunger, Harold Suter, and Wally Kroeker, *Faith Dilemmas for Marketplace Christians*, (Scottsdale, Pennsylvania: Herald Press, 1997), pp. 17-18.

2 Elizabeth Jeffries, "*Your Work: A Job or a Calling?*" *Sunday/Monday Woman* 2:5, September/October 2001, p. 37.

Chapter 6: Sunday and Monday in Sync

1 William Diehl, *Ministry in Daily Life: A Practical Guide for Congregations*, (Washington, D.C.: The Alban Institute, 1996), p. 92.

2 Robert Eynon, "Faith Odysseys in Progress." in *Partners in the Spirit* (Northeastern Pennsylvania Synod, ELCA, January 2002), p. 7.

Bibliography

Banks, Robert J., ed. 1993. *Faith Goes to Work: Reflections from the Marketplace.* Washington, D. C.: The Alban Institute.

Dickhart, Judith McWilliams. 2002. *Church-going Insider or Gospel-carrying Outsider? A Different View of Congregations.* Chicago: Evangelical Lutheran Church in America Division for Ministry.

Diehl, William. 1996. *Ministry in Daily Life: A Practical Guide for Congregations.* Washington, D.C.: The Alban Institute.

Dozier, Verna J., ed. 1988. *The Calling of the Laity: Verna Dozier's Anthology.* Washington, D. C.: The Alban Institute.

Everist, Norma Cook and Nelvin Vos. 1996. *Where in the World Are You? Connecting Faith and Daily Life.* Washington, D. C.: The Alban Institute.

Faith @ Work. A quarterly magazine published by Faith At Work, Inc., 106 E Broad St., #B, Falls Church, VA, 22046-4501.

Jacobsen, Steve. 1997. *Hearts to God, Hands to Work: Connecting Spirituality and Work.* Washington, D. C.: The Alban Institute.

Kolden, Marc. 1994. "Work and Meaning: Some Theological Reflections," *Interpretation* 48, no. 3 (July): 262-271.

Nash, Laura and McLennan, Scotty. 2001. *Church on Sunday, work on Monday: The Challenge of Fusing Christian Values with Business Life.* San Francisco: Jossey-Bass.

Page, Patricia. 1993. *All God's People Are Ministers: Equipping Church Members for Ministry.* Minneapolis: Augsburg Books.

Pierce, Gregory F. A. 2001. *Spirituality @ Work: 10 Ways to Balance Your Life at Work.* Chicago: Loyola Press.

Weiser, Carol, ed. 1995. *Working: Making a Difference in God's World. Sourcebook.* Chicago: Evangelical Lutheran Church in America.

Wingren, Gustaf. 1957. *Luther on Vocation.* Philadelphia: Muhlenberg Press.

Internet sites

The Episcopal Church in the U. S. A., *Ministry in Daily Life* page. http://episcopalchurch.org/ministry/daily.htm

The Evangelical Lutheran Church in America, Division for Ministry, *Ministry in Daily Life* page. http://www.elca.org/dm/midl/ministry.html

InterVarsity Christian Fellowship/USA, *Ministry in Daily Life* page. http://www.ivmdl.org/